Seafood
M·I·C·R·O·W·A·V·E
C·O·O·K·E·R·Y

Seafood

M·I·C·R·O·W·A·V·E

C·O·O·K·E·R·Y

JOANNA FARROW

GRUB STREET • LONDON

Published by
Grub Street
Golden House
28–31 Great Pulteney Street
London W1

Photographs by Paul Grater
Food prepared and styled for photography
by Joanna Farrow
Step-by-step and fish illustrations by Andrea Dharlow and
Graeme Andrew

Farrow, Joanna
   Seafood microwave cookery.
   1. Cookery (Fish) 2. Microwave cookery
   I. Title
   641.6'92   TX747

ISBN 0–948817–10–0
ISBN 0–948817–11–9 Pbk

Typeset by Chapterhouse, The Cloisters, Formby
Printed and bound in Great Britain by
R J Acford, Chichester

I would like to thank my sister, Celia, for
typing the manuscript and all my family for
trying out the recipes, particularly my
husband, Nick who lived on fish alone for
several months.

FOREWORD

I have been fascinated by fish ever since we, as a family netted shrimps on holiday and watched them turn from semi-transparency to the beautiful coral fleshed delicacy with the sweet, salty taste. This enthusiasm is for all fish, from the humble herring to the far-away, exotic species that only occasionally make their way to British markets. I love the versatility of fish – there are over sixty types available on the fishmonger's slab and many different ways of cooking each. I love the simplicity with which stunning recipes can be created and best of all, I love my most recent discovery – it's total compatibility with the microwave method of cooking.

The reasons for this rapport are many. The fish is cooked so quickly that it retains its natural juices and texture, resulting in a flavour that's undisputedly superior to conventionally cooked fish. No cooking liquid is necessary, so again the fish retains flavour as well as valuable nutrients. Unlike meat, fish does not need to brown to look appetising, nor does it need gentle cooking to tenderise, a task which only the conventional oven does well. It is also easy – delicate pieces of cooked fish which would normally break up as you precariously manoeuvre them from the pan, can be cooked on the serving plate – altogether a gentler approach for one of the most fragile foods. Two other well known, but none-the-less excellent attributes of the microwave is its ability to defrost, and to reheat without toughening up. This is particularly useful for ready cooked shellfish which can turn disappointingly 'chewy' when conventionally reheated. Good news for late diners!

I am as keen to encourage people to enjoy good, fresh fish as I am for them to microwave it. Not simply as a once a week (or less!) ritual but as an important part of any diet, everyday or otherwise. For entertaining, fish should not serve purely as an appetising starter but as an exciting alternative to meat for a main course. For this reason I have 'star marked' all those recipes which I think are most suitable for a special occasion. Having said this, none of the recipes in this book are too humble to offer guests. Use it purely as a guide.

Finally, for our microwave exploits to be praiseworthy we must rely on a good supply of the raw material. The sale of fresh fish suffered a slump due to lack of demand but is now enjoying a resurgence, both in independent outlets and through supermarket wet-fish counters. I hope, that with the ever increasing number of microwave owners, this book serves well in marrying a perfect partnership.

AT A GLANCE
MENU PLANNER

A–Z OF SEAFOOD

9

INTRODUCTION

STOCKS AND SAUCES

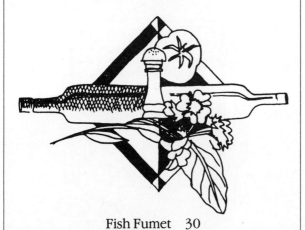

SOUPS AND STARTERS

SNACKS AND LIGHT MEALS FOR ONE AND TWO

MAIN COURSES

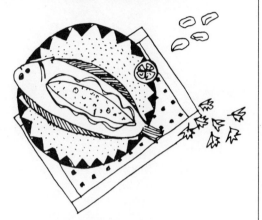

SIDE DISHES

A–Z OF SEAFOOD

Anchovy

Long, slender and silver sheened, the fresh anchovy bears little resemblance to its canned counterpart which plays a substantial role in many fish dishes. Instead, enjoy the fresh fish as you would a plateful of sardines, or use as garnish with a special seafood pizza. 'Essence' of anchovy, a thick bottled sauce is invaluable for zipping up blander fish dishes.

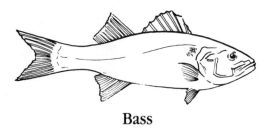

Bass

In the same league as salmon and sole, this stunning, densely fleshed fish makes a magnificent main course for a special meal. A whole specimen of about 1⅓ kg (3 lb) can be cooked like salmon, whereas larger fish, cut into steaks, are best served with a garlicky tomato or wine sauce.

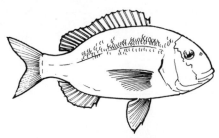

Bream (Sea)

The sea bream comes in many different guises – red or black (and many different shades in between) and firm or soft fleshed. Reasonably priced, it is worth experimenting with but cook 'dry' rather than swamping with sauces. Spicy bastes and oriental-style marinades enliven its sometimes mild taste.

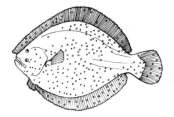

Brill

A smaller, inferior cousin to turbot, brill is variable in price and availability so buy when given the chance. A whole fish of about 1⅓ kg (3 lb) fits snugly onto a microwave turntable, for poaching and serving with any Bechamel-based sauce. Like turbot, fish stews and soups gain a velvety texture from its gelatinous bones.

Clams

The huge brown clams most commonly seen at the fishmongers have thick coarse shells which stubbornly resist being wrenched apart. But the microwave performs this task with ease, releasing the rich meat for mincing into chowders. The petite and delicate 'Venus' clams on the other hand, open in seconds and give a sweetly salt taste to pasta dishes and seafood salads. A rarity on the fishmonger's slab, they are worth buying impromptu – even a small cluster makes a pretty garnish for any simply cooked piece of fish.

Cockles

Despite their abundance, ready cooked, alongside winkles and whelks on every seaside fish stall, cockles in their shells are pretty hard to come by. Microwave until opened and eat from the shells or use the flesh to colour an everyday fish pie – an equally good use for jars of cockles in brine.

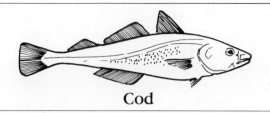

Cod

King of the rambling cod family is the great cod itself. Freshly cooked, it falls into succulent flakes to reveal a fine white 'curd'. This indicates total freshness, but sadly much of the cod sold is already past its prime. Available in steaks, cutlets and fillets, cod microwaves beautifully and is highly versatile. Flake into fish pies, fish cakes or hotpots or dress up poached pieces with parsley, mushroom, cheese or tomato sauce. A small codling weighing up to about $1\frac{3}{4}$ kg ($3\frac{1}{2}$ lb) can be cooked whole like salmon.

Cod fillets can also be bought smoked like haddock, or salted and dried to prolong storage life. The large roes, sliced and sautéed in butter make a nourishing meal, but are most often seen ready-smoked for making into taramasalata.

Coley

The humble coley, once relegated to the cat's bowl is making a rightful comeback to family meals. Like cod but more coarse and grey it turns pleasantly white when cooked, so is worth exploiting the bargain price. Flake into pies and any dishes which will disguise its identity – only a connoisseur will distinguish it from cod.

Conger Eel

No relation to the finer freshwater eel, this full-time seafarer provides an economical family meal given ample cooking to release the meaty white flesh from the profusion of bones. These bones and thick skin can be offputting but need not bother 'cook' nor diner if the eel is used to flavour stews in which both are discarded before eating. An excellent substitute for more expensive white fish in a 'Matelote'.

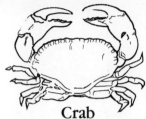

Crab

Deliciously rich and meaty, plenteous and so inexpensive, crab can be relished for everyday eating. Although obtainable ready dressed or as 'blocks' of frozen meat, dressing a crab is a therapeutic, rewarding exercise which leaves the shell for a serving dish or to flavour stocks for bisque. Don't be afraid of putting the shell in the microwave – neither will explode!

Crab-flavoured 'ocean sticks' and canned crab are always easy to buy, but substitute for the real thing only as a last resort.

Crawfish

(Spiny Lobster, Crayfish)

Almost as good as the lobster itself but lacking the meaty claws, the crawfish should be killed, cooked and served in the same way. Small crawfish tails are frequently sold frozen – good for salads or microwaving in garlic butter. (Don't confuse with the freshwater, miniature crayfish – which is taken from rivers).

Dab

A rough-skinned member of the plaice family that's generally too small to bother dressing up. Instead use as a convenient light meal for one or two, dotted with butter, microwaved (very briefly) and served with seasoning and a drizzle of lemon.

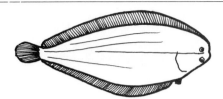

Dover Sole

Potential sole buyers may be put off by its extortionate price, but if one per portion is out of the question, a couple of fillets in a creamy seafood sauce might make this highly desirable flat fish a feasible choice for a special meal. Avoid swamping with elaborate accompaniments that will overpower the delicate flavour and firm white flesh. Dover sole responds far better to sensitive treatment.

Dublin Bay Prawns

(Scampi, Norway Lobster, Langoustine).

This beautiful, coral pink crustacean conceals a relatively small amount of flesh (the long slender claws are not eaten) so, in terms of meat per pound they are pretty expensive. However, one or two make an exotic garnish for a salad or plain cooked cutlet.

Eel

Don't let visions of 'eels with green liquer and mash' or 'Jellied eels' deter you from trying this highly esteemed fish. After skinning and chopping into manageable-sized pieces the flesh can be simmered in wine, stock or cider, or puréed into mousses for a deliciously meaty meal. Baby 'elvers' or 'bootlace eels' are traditionally fried, a technique that's best reserved for the frying pan.

Always buy live eels as they spoil quickly. Squeamish cooks should ask the fishmonger to kill and skin the eels as their reflexes make them wriggle frantically.

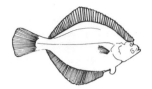

Flounder

Like other cheap flat fish flounder makes a marvellously easy meal, buttered and microwaved on its serving plate and accompanied by a parsley or tartare sauce. Gastronomically however it has an 'average' reputation, because of its coarse flavour and soft flesh.

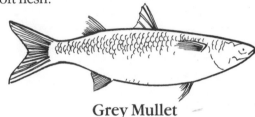

Grey Mullet

No relation to the smaller red mullet this 'metallic' skinned fish is one of the more affordable, rarer species. Best cooked without liquid and dressed up with tomatoes, herbs, fennel or pernod. The superb roe (which is the *real* one for Taramasalata) can be added to stuffings for extra flavour.

Thick and coarse, any stray scales could easily ruin a potentially good dish, so thoroughly remove before cooking.

Gurnard

Fairly rare but invitingly cheap, this prehistoric looking fish is generally reserved for flavouring fish soups. The red gurnard is the finest for flavour but should not be confused with the superior red mullet.

Haddock

It takes a discerning diner to distinguish the difference between haddock and cod, so wise shoppers will plump for the cheapest of the two (generally haddock costs slightly more). Sold in the same cuts as cod, it is totally interchangeable in any recipe.

Smoked Finnan Haddock has done far more for the reputation of this fish. Originally cured over seaweed in the Scottish village of Findon, it is now commercially imitated with cheap dyes, and lacks the flavour of the true article. Many fishmongers sell both, so you can compare colour and price for yourself.

Arbroath smokies are another Scottish speciality. Here, small whole haddock are beheaded and gutted (but not split) and hot-smoked so they are ready for eating. The dark skin reveals a golden flesh that is improved by briefly warming through.

Hake

This deep water member of the cod family is unfortunately fairly rare. Sold whole or in fillets and steaks, hake can be cooked and served like cod, or poached and steeped in a Mediterranean-style herby marinade for serving cold. Hake contains few bones – quite a consideration for fussy eaters.

Halibut

This enormous flat fish is always sold in steaks unless you buy a small chicken halibut at just 900 g–1½ kg (2–3 lb) which, like brill and chicken turbot, may just squeeze whole into the microwave. Halibut does not aspire to the superior taste of turbot but is none the less highly prized for its delicate flavour and firm flesh. Only its tendency to dryness reduces its popularity, although the microwave copes with this marvellously.

Smoked halibut makes a delicious alternative to smoked cod or haddock.

Herring

Over fishing led this popular buy to scarcity and hence restrictions on fishing. But now it is back in glorious abundance, as cheap and tasty as ever. A distinctly flavoured fish, rich in oil and extremely nutritious, herrings are best baked whole with little embellishment.

There are many ways of curing herrings from simply 'sousing' to the various forms of smoking. Kippers are split, cold smoked herring which need further cooking before serving. Bloaters (smoked ungutted for a gamey flavour) also need further cooking whereas the Buckling is hot – smoked ready for eating cold, although a few seconds in the microwave brings out its full flavour.

Huss (Flake, Rigg, dogfish)

A cheap, mushy fleshed fish that is most frequently bought fried in batter from the 'chippi', under the misleading name of Rock Salmon. Despite its many aliases, huss is easily identified by its pinky grey colour and 'log'-like shape, once filleted. Not good enough to eat plain but a worthy addition to fish pies and fish cakes.

John Dory

Easily identified by its huge head, flat body and dark spot on each flank, the John Dory is renowned as a classic ingredient in Bouillabaisse and other fish stews. Larger fish, although difficult to fillet, make an excellent substitute in turbot or sole recipes.

Lemon Sole

Not a true sole but still a delicious fish that outshines the freshest plaice and provides a worthy substitute for Dover sole.

The 'lemon' refers to the tinge of colour on the skin, rather than the flavour which is pleasantly delicate.

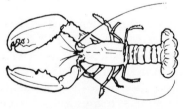

Lobster

The ultimate taste in seafood, perhaps the ultimate taste in food? Certainly for most of us it is a luxury we rarely indulge in, so buying 'fresh' is imperative. This means choosing a 'live' lobster and cooking it yourself. The best way is to place the lobster in a pan of cold water and cover with a tight fitting lid. Bring to the boil, then allow 15 minutes for the first 450 g (1 lb) and 10 minutes for any extra. (By the time the water is hot the lobster has

expired painlessly). However, if you find this idea repugnant buy ready-cooked, but only from a reputable source.

The choice of recipe can make or break your prized catch. Many of the 'classics' drown the flesh in heavy cheese and overpowering spicy sauces. Instead treat your lobster with subtle sophistication – a splash of cream and a hint of brandy is unbeatable.

Mackerel

Steely blue and banded with black markings, this underrated fish is undoubtedly one of the most beautiful. Very oily (and as meaty as its relative the tuna) mackerel benefits from, in fact *needs* tangy embellishments to lighten the intense flavour. 'Gooseberry sauce' is the famous example but orange, mustard, sorrel and horseradish work equally well. Choose the smallest specimens on sale – none but the heartiest appetites can cope with a large fish.

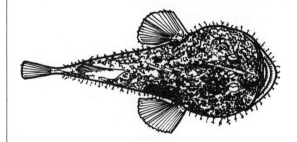

Monkfish

Only in recent years has this superb fish risen from virtual obscurity to pride of place on the fishmonger's slab. It is usually only the tail piece that we buy – the hideously huge head is already discarded, perhaps to encourage sales! Classified as white yet with a texture and flavour more akin to shellfish, monkfish is delicious cubed and sautéed or baked in the piece. Either way, microwave until barely tender. Overcooking gives a disappointingly tough and shrunken flesh.

Look out for smoked monkfish, a fairly recent innovation.

Mussels

Nothing quite gets the mouth watering like a bowl of hot, steaming mussels. Equally inviting is their price and ease of cooking, particularly in the microwave. Placed in a covered bowl (no liquid is necessary) the shells gradually gape open to reveal the beautiful saffron-coloured flesh. Garlicky tomato sauces, rich creamy ones or simply flavoured butters enhance their sweet, salty flavour. Serve as a starter, main course or stunning garnish for other shellfish dishes.

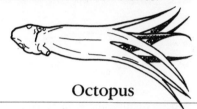

Octopus

There are two steps to ensuring success with cooking an octopus. Firstly 'ninety-nine bashings' (presumably on a board with a mallet) is said to be necessary to tenderise its toughness. Perhaps a more useful guideline is to beat the octopus until it has lost its 'spring'. Let the fishmonger advise you on this.

The second step is a preliminary cooking. Unfortunately the microwave does not cook sufficiently slowly to do this successfully so use the conventional oven. Afterwards the firm but sweetly tender pieces of flesh can be simmered in stews with tomatoes or wine, or tossed in seafood salads.

Oysters

Once the food of the poor, overfishing and scarcity have made oysters the luxury they are today. Those from Whitstable and Colchester have the finest reputation in Europe (only to be eaten raw!) but the Portuguese ones make a superb creamy stew that's prepared in mere minutes. Oysters are much more plentiful in the Southen Hemisphere however.

Pilchards

Officially defined as a sardine over 7½ cm (3 in) long, although they're usually still labelled 'sardines' at the fishmongers. Prepare and serve hot or cold as you would sardines.

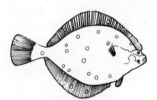

Plaice

It may be inferior to sole, but plaice is still Britain's favourite flat fish. Whole ones, like other flatfish, can only be microwaved one or two at a time but at the cooking speed (about 2 minutes each) this is still feasible for family meals. Fillets may be served with a parsley, cheese or mustard sauce or simply with savoury butter. Judge quality by the spots – the more vivid the fresher the catch.

Prawns and Shrimps

The difference between a prawn and a shrimp is purely one of size, and both names cover a multitude of species. Firstly, there is the common prawn that must be bought whole, and freshly peeled to enjoy the true flavour. Then there are the tiny pink or brown shrimps that are so good potted, and the luxuriously expensive king prawns that are the meatiest and strongest flavoured of the lot.

All are sweet, succulent and delicious when fresh but avoid buying frozen or worse still peeled frozen prawns that have been thawed for sale on the 'deli' counter. If given the chance buy raw prawns (identified by their greyish colouring) and microwave in a little butter. You will never want to revert to buying cooked.

Red Mullet

These small, pretty fish can be excellent if fresh, tasteless if not, so choose carefully. The redder and moister the skin the more likely it is to be tasty. Usually cooked without liquid, Red Mullet is enhanced by fennel, Pernod, herbs and garlic and any Mediterranean-type ingredients. Serve as a stylish main course.

Red Snapper

Native to South Atlantic waters, you will have to shop around for this beautiful red tinged fish. Firm fleshed and well flavoured, it can be stuffed with herbs and garlic or used in place of bream or bass. Before cooking be sure to remove its armour plating of scales.

Red Haddock (Redfish)

Another red skinned fish, this one has very large eyes and a white flesh which falls into large flakes rather like cod or haddock. Usually reasonably priced redfish can be baked whole, simply with savoury butter or basted with an oriental or spicy marinade.

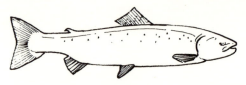

Salmon

Many of the world's rivers and oceans abound with this handsome fish but it is those that are spawned in the upper reaches of Scotland's rivers that are most esteemed for quality and flavour. Scottish salmon farming has done a lot to deflate the price of salmon so that we can all, if only once in a while relish this uniquely flavoured, regal fish. Cook whole or in steaks until the colour just turns opaque. Overcooked salmon quickly dries out.

Salmon Trout (Sea Trout)

Combining the superb flavour of salmon with the moister texture of trout the salmon trout is, not surprisingly, even more highly regarded than the salmon itself. Prepare and cook in exactly the same way as you would salmon.

Sardines

Canned sardines, however nourishing and convenient, compare infavourably with the fresh specimen. Rich and oily they make an easy summertime meal, cooked in butter, served with tomatoes or steeped in a flavoured dressing.

Scallops

Enclosed in a beautiful shell the delicately flavoured, tender scallop is one of the most highly regarded of all shellfish – with a price to match! Fortunately a few go a long way whether you skewer them with cheaper fish or pile back into their shells after cooking and bathe in a creamy sauce. Scallops need a mere flash in the microwave – overcooking renders them tough and, hence, a waste of money.

Shark

Meatiest of the meaty fish, serve shark steaks and your guests might think they're eating chicken! Often available in the freezer cabinet of adventurous fishmongers, shark provides an interesting culinary experience. Marinate in herby flavoured oils before cooking, or dot with butter to counteract the dryish texture.

Sprats

Worth buying for their price alone. These tiny silvery fish only warrant simple cooking. Flashed in the browning dish and drizzled with lemon and seasoning they make a light family tea. Smoked sprats, a Scandinavian speciality, are equally tempting.

Squid

Heaped fritters of squid or 'calamari' on a Spanish holiday are what get many of us hooked on this strange sea creature. Preparation is easy but messy, so squeamish cooks may prefer to buy ready cleaned squid, now on sale at some supermarkets and fishmongers. Highly versatile, it can be stuffed, fried or tossed in salads. Also essential in a good Paella.

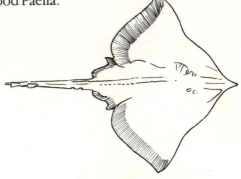

Skate

Skate is a cartilaginous fish. In other words, like huss and monkfish it contains no brittle bones and the flesh falls away from the cartilage with ease. Frying in the browning dish with butter and capers is the microwave method to a classic dish but it is also good shredded into salads.

Skate 'knobs' cut from the tail are sometimes available. Add these to pies or stews.

Swordfish

Like shark, swordfish makes a pretty meaty meal and requires the same moist cooking to reduce its tendancy to dryness. Turning the thoroughly dried steaks in the browning dish produces an appetisingly seared surface. Don't be put off buying frozen, it is often only available in this state and tastes surprisingly good.

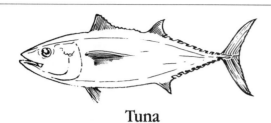

Tuna

Scarlet red and moist, a fresh piece of tuna resembles a joint of beef far more than fish but pales during cooking to a colour similar to that of canned. Cook lightly with garlic, butter and herbs or use in a rich casserole. Bonito, a smaller relative makes a worthy substitute.

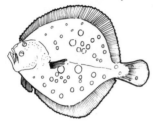

Turbot

Turbot is considered one of the finest of seafoods and can certainly compete with the best of them. As delicately flavoured as sole, it has a firmer, meatier texture. Although turbot grows to a colossal size (and is usually bought as steaks) a small chicken turbot can be cooked whole like brill. Serve with a shellfish, prawn, parsley or hollandaise sauce or combine with shellfish in a delicious mousse.

Witch

Resembling a miniature Dover sole, Witch suits the same cooking methods. Don't be fooled however when buying as witch has an inferior flavour and should be priced accordingly.

Whitebait

A tiny, oily fish that should only be bought absolutely fresh as it is cooked and eaten ungutted. Frozen whitebait makes a good buy but has little value in the microwave as it is best fried. Very large whitebait however can be cooked as for sprats.

Whiting

A softer textured and small cousin of the cod, whiting is bought in fillets, or whole if small. Besides coley it is the cheapest of the white fish and infinitely useful as a substitute for cod. Fresh whiting spoils very quickly so opt for frozen if the fresh looks limp and dull.

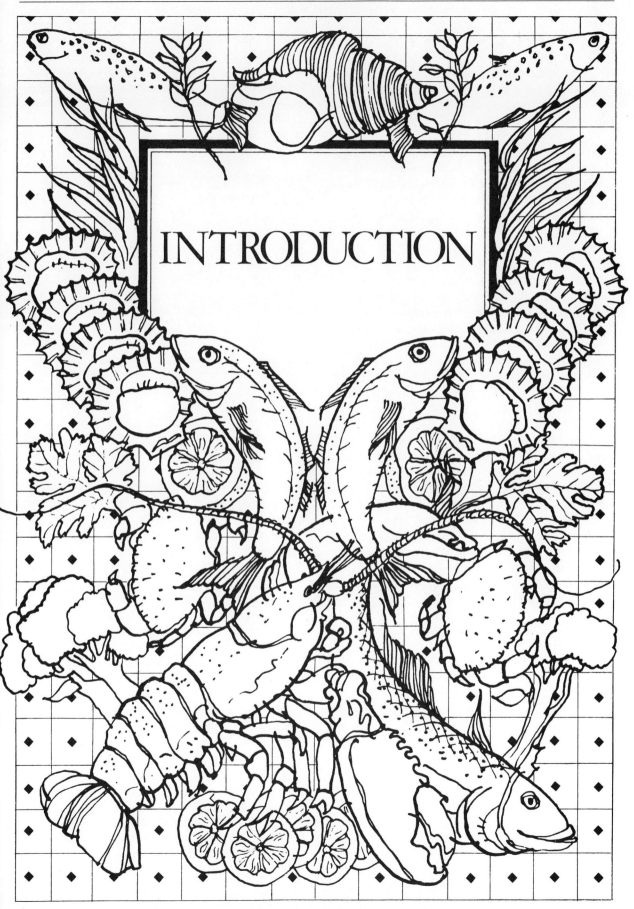

INTRODUCTION

UNDERSTANDING MICROWAVES

Inside the microwave, electrical energy from the mains supply is converted by a magnetron into electromagnetic, high-frequency waves. These waves are attracted to the water molecules in food causing such a rapid vibration (billions of times a second) that the heat generated is sufficient to cook the food.

Microwave energy cannot penetrate the metal lining of the microwave cavity. The door, although transparent is lined with a fine metal mesh which prevents microwaves passing through. Any microwave energy that hits the walls or door is deflected back to the food. If the door is opened during cooking microwave energy is automatically cut out, so provided it has not been damaged or tampered with a microwave oven is completely safe to use.

Like all electrical gadgets microwave ovens are becoming increasingly more sophisticated. Browning elements, temperature probes, electronic programming, humidity detectors and combination ovens (a microwave and conventional cooker in one) are but a few of the modifications now widely available. However a basic model will actually cook the food just as well and for this reason most people start with a basic model and advance to the more luxurious ones.

Power settings

Microwave ovens vary in power output (ie the wattage). Most domestic microwaves have a power output of 600 to 700 watts, but some are as low as 350 watts. This wattage (which is indicated in the instruction manual, and should be researched before buying) determines the speed of cooking. The higher the wattage the shorter the time.

In order to achieve different cooking speeds, each microwave has variable power settings (just like a conventional cooker). Some models have numerous different settings such as, 'bake', 'simmer', 'roast' etc but the three most useful settings, and those included on

basic models are LOW, MEDIUM and HIGH. In this book high refers to 650 watts or 100 per cent full power, MEDIUM to 50 per cent of the full power and LOW to 30 per cent of the full power. If your oven is lower than 650 watts add a little extra cooking time, if it is higher deduct a little cooking time.

Containers and special equipment

Never use metal dishes. Microwave energy is deflected by metal, not only leaving the food uncooked but more than likely damaging the magnetron. Likewise plates and dishes with metalic decoration should be avoided.

Unless your model advises against it, small amounts of kitchen foil can be used to protect areas of food from overcooking.

Aside from these materials almost any other can be used. Microwave energy passes through china, glass, polythene containers, paper plates and wood, so buying a stack of special equipment is unnecessary. However a few lightweight microwave dishes are infinitely useful. On sale in department and kitchen stores, they come in many shapes and sizes, and most are both freezer and dishwasher proof. To test whether your own container or bowl is suitable for microwaving place in the microwave, and put a glass of water inside it. Microwave for 1–2 minutes. If the water is hot but the dish stays cool then it is suitable. If both dish and water become warm then it is usable, but cooking will take longer. If the dish becomes hot and the water stays cool then the dish is absorbing too much microwave energy and should not be used.

The shape of the container plays an equally important role in microwaving. Round or oval containers are better than square as they have no corners in which microwave energy can gather and overcook. Shallow dishes are better than deep as the energy only penetrates to a depth of about 5 cm (2 in). This means that food in the centre of a large container cooks by heat conduction rather than microwave energy so the food would need to be stirred several times to ensure that it is evenly cooked. If a recipe requires plenty of milk, or mussels, etc which rise as they heat up, use a container which they will only half fill when put into the oven.

COOKING FISH IN THE MICROWAVE

Fish is one of the easiest and most successfully microwaved foods. But to achieve the best possible results the following techniques must be observed.

Covering food before cooking

Unless a recipe states otherwise, the container should always be covered so that steam and moisture are trapped. Unless your container has its own lid, use cling film which enables you to see the food through it. Leave a small area uncovered on one edge of the dish to prevent a build up of pressure. This also enables you to stir the contents of the dish without having to renew the cling film.

Take care when removing the lid or cling film. Open away from you to prevent scalding your hands.

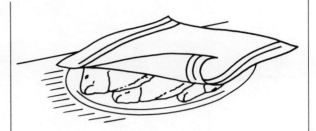

Kitchen paper makes a better covering for foods that you do not want to turn soggy during cooking, eg bacon, wrapped fish and bread, or rolls. Remove immediately after cooking to prevent it from sticking to the food.

Scoring whole fish

Unless a recipe states otherwise, score whole fish diagonally through the skin on both sides to prevent it from splitting during cooking. This is not necessary for very small fish like sprats or sardines.

Arranging fish

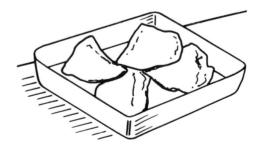

The greater the surface area that is exposed, the quicker and more evenly the fish cooks so careful arrangement will ensure good results. Arrange fish fillets in a large shallow dish with the thickest parts to the outside, overlapping the tail ends in the centre of the dish.

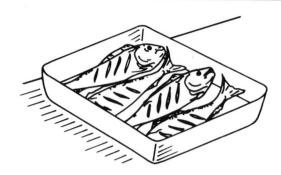

If cooking more than one whole fish arrange the fish, side by side, in the container alternating the direction of the heads.

Fishcakes and roulades should be arranged in a circle on a plate. If it is necessary to have any in the centre of the plate, swap with those near the edge of the dish during cooking.

Very small whole fish can be arranged in a sunburst fashion, heads on the outside, on a large flat plate. Cook all fish whether whole or filleted in a single layer.

Stirring, turning and re-arranging fish

To ensure even cooking the fish, or ingredients, are re-positioned during cooking. Stirring applies to stews, soups and stir fries, or any recipe which is largely liquid, or easily stirred without breaking up. Spoon the pieces of food in the middle of the container to the outside and vice versa.

Fillets, steaks and whole fish can be turned over during cooking to give the underside a better chance to cook. Some fish, particularly flat fish, can become damaged and look less presentable if turned over. These are best left in their original position.

If cooking several whole fish, re-arrange half way through cooking so that those on the inside are moved to the outside and vice versa.

Standing time

All microwaved food continues to cook after removing from the oven so a 'standing time' is allowed in which the dish can complete cooking, and the heat distribution can equalise itself. Any dish that requires a standing time of more than two minutes should be covered with foil.

Using a browning dish

Although the flesh of fish does not actually brown during cooking, a browning dish is a worthwhile investment for cooking stir fries, fishcakes and any recipe that benefits from a 'seared' surface or browned finish. The browning dish is first preheated in the microwave (following the manufacturer's specified time) before the food is added. Once the sizzling dies down the recipe can be completed in the browning dish.

Testing whether fish is cooked

Always microwave fish for a little less time than the recipe states. Prod the thickest area with a fork. If the flesh 'flakes' and has turned from translucent to opaque it is ready to remove from the oven. Remember that it will cook a little more during the standing time, and you can always pop it back in the microwave if it needs a moment longer.

Defrosting in the microwave

Frozen fish for stews, and soups, or fish that is to be pureed or flaked in recipes can be successfully cooked from frozen. But fish that is to be served 'in the piece' should be thawed

DEFROSTING FISH AND SHELLFISH

MICROWAVING TIMES ON LOW

FISH	DEFROSTING TIME	DEFROSTING TIPS	STANDING TIME
White fish cutlets, steaks, fillets (eg cod, haddock, halibut) or whole flat fish (eg sole, plaice) per 450 g (1 lb)	5–6 min	Position thickest parts towards edge of dish and re-arrange during defrosting. If stuck together break apart as soon as possible to speed up defrosting. Shield any areas which start to get warm with small pieces of foil	5 min
Oily fish, whole or fillets (eg mackerel, herring, sardine) per 450 g (1 lb)	7–8 min	Turn fish over halfway through defrosting and re-arrange if defrosting more than two. Shield any areas which start to get warm with small pieces of foil	5 min
Smoked fish fillets (eg kippers, mackerel) per 225 g (8 oz)	2–3 min	As for white fish, cutlets, steaks and fillets	3 min
Meaty fish steaks (eg swordfish, shark, tuna) per 450 g (1 lb)	6–7 min	As for white fish, cutlets, steaks and fillets	5 min
Whole prawns, shrimps per 225 g (8 oz)	3–4 min	Arrange on a plate, leaving centre clear. Re-arrange during defrosting	5 min
Peeled prawns, shrimps, scampi per 225 g (8 oz)	3–4 min	Remove from bags and place on a plate, leaving centre clear	3 min
per 100 g (4 oz)	2½ min	Cover with absorbent paper. Turn gently and drain off any excess water	2 min
Scallops per 225 g (8 oz)	3–4 min	As for peeled prawns, shrimps, and scampi	3 min
Crabmeat per 225 g (8 oz) block	3½–4 min	Remove outer pieces from oven as soon as they are defrosted	2 min
Crab claws, crayfish tails, etc per 225 g (8 oz)	4–5 min	Re-arrange several times during defrosting	5 min

NB Large white or oily fish are best defrosted in the refrigerator. Otherwise microwave on LOW at 2-minute intervals, leaving a 5-minute rest between each one and watching carefully for areas which start to get warm. Shield these with small pieces of foil.

first, otherwise the outside will be cooked while the inside is still icy. Arrange fish as you would for cooking and cover with cling film. Microwave on LOW for the time stated on the chart, turning and re-arranging as you would when cooking fish. If the fish is frozen in 'block' form, break off the thawed pieces from the outside as soon as they are defrosted.

NB Certain fish dishes should not be attempted in the microwave. These include battered and breadcrumbed fish (which will not crisp) and any deep fried recipes as you have no control over the temperature of the oil.

COOKING FISH AND SHELLFISH

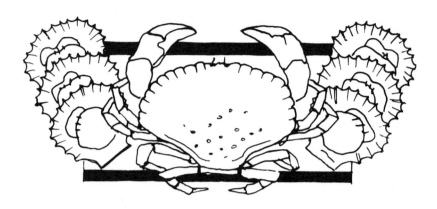

MICROWAVING TIMES ON HIGH

FISH	COOKING TIME	COOKING TIPS	STANDING TIME
Cutlets, steaks, fillets (eg cod, haddock, halibut, coley, salmon) per 450 g (1 lb)	4–5 min	Position thickest parts towards edges of dish. Re-arrange during cooking	4–5 min
Whole flat fish (eg sole, plaice, brill) per 450 g (1 lb)	3–4 min	Remove fins and place on buttered plate. Score skin. Shield tails with small pieces of foil if beginning to overcook	3 min
Whole round fish (eg whiting, sardines, mullet, mackerel, herring) per 450 g (1 lb)	3–4 min	Score skin of larger fish. Turn over fish half way through cooking and re-arrange if cooking more than two. Shield tails with small pieces of foil if beginning to overcook	4–5 min
Smoked fish fillets (eg haddock, cod, kippers) per 450 g (1 lb)	4–5 min	Position thickest parts towards edges of dish. Re-arrange during cooking	4–5 min
Scallops per 225 g (8 oz)	1 min	Pat dry, halve if large, toss in melted butter	
Mussels and small clams per 1.2 litres (2 pints)	4 minutes, remove opened shells. Cook remainder for further 2 minutes. Discard any unopened shells	Place in a bowl with 75 ml/3fl oz stock and sprinkling of black pepper	
Squid per 225 g (8 oz)	45 seconds – 1 min	Prepare and cut into rings. Toss in melted butter. Stir once during cooking	
Dublin Bay Prawns (8) Live	2 min	Place in a large bowl. Quickly pour on enough boiling water to just cover. Cover bowl before cooking	3 min
(8) Ready killed	2 min	Space apart on a large flat dish, cover. Re-arrange during cooking	3 min

BUYING FISH

Choosing

Only buy the *freshest* fish. Whole specimens should have a glossy sheen with eyes that are bright, not sunken and dull. The skin should be firm and taught when prodded and the flesh succulent looking and moist. Any fish that naturally display vivid colours or markings should be bought in this way. Paling can indicate staleness. The general aroma should be of the sea – certainly not dead fish!

Lobster and crab should feel weighty for their size and have both claws intact. When shaken you should hear no sound of water.

Mussels, clams, cockles and scallops are best avoided on a very hot day, particularly if many of the shells are gaping open.

Prawns and shrimps should have richly coloured firm shells, and heads intact. Avoid any that look as though they have been squashed.

If you are not able to buy fresh or the fresh looks unappetising, take a look in the supermarket freezer cabinet. Frozen fish is not ideal, but certainly beats fresh of dubious quality. Look for undamaged packs and solidly frozen fish. Dull white patches indicate 'freezer burn' due to staleness or poor freezing conditions.

Storing

It goes without saying that all fresh fish should be eaten as soon as possible after purchase. Only smoked fish stores well for a couple of days.

Clean and gut fish as soon as you get it home, and to avoid a double-dose of fishy hands, skin, fillet or chop as your recipe requires. Refrigerate until ready to cook on a plate, loosely covered with foil or cling film is best.

Shellfish should be eaten on the day of purchase. Place mussels, clams and cockles in a bowl of water with a sprinkling of flour or oatmeal. (This helps them clean their digestive tracts.) Oysters should be chilled on a tray with their rounded shells face down to retain the salty juices. All crustaceans can be chilled on a tray until ready to use and if live, placed in the salad drawer.

PREPARING FISH

Provided you do not choose the busiest time of the week, any good fishmonger will fillet, skin or simply clean your chosen fish – all in a fraction of the time it takes most cooks to do at home. However, performing these tasks at home, or at least knowing how to is infinitely useful.

Select a good sharp knife, your sturdiest chopping board and follow the directions below, not forgetting to throw the scraps in the stockpot to get maximum value from every scrap.

Cleaning and gutting round fish

(eg herring, mackerel or hake)

Scale the fish by running a knife close to the skin from head to tail end.

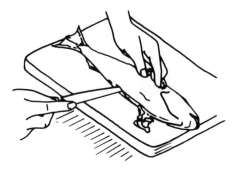

A. Using a sharp knife slit open the belly and scrape out the intestines.

B. Rinse the fish well, inside and out, under cold running water.

Filleting flat fish

(eg sole, plaice)

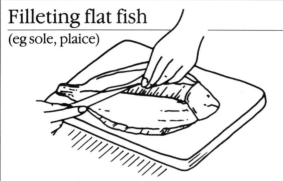

Make a slit through the backbone of fish from head to tail. Slip a knife sideways against bone and using short sharp strokes, lift the fillet free from bone.

Cut off the fillet at tail end to remove completely. Remove the remaining three fillets in the same way.

Skinning fillets

(eg cod, haddock, sole)

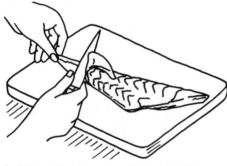

Lay fish, skin side down on a board. Dip fingers of one hand in salt and grip tail end. With other hand slip a knife in between skin and flesh and saw flesh away from skin.

Boning a round fish

(eg sardines, herrings)

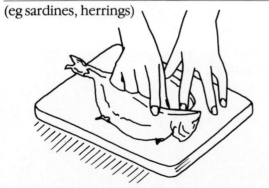

A. Clean and gut the fish and cut off head and fins. Continue the cut made in belly down to

the tail. Open out fish and press firmly along backbone with the thumb so that you can feel the backbone coming away from the flesh.

B. Turn fish over and lift out backbone and any loose bones.

Cleaning squid

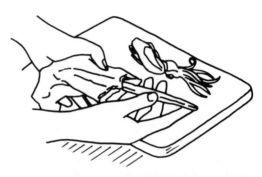

A. Pull the head and tentacles away from the body. Slip finger into the body cavity and pull out the transparent cartilage or 'quill' and any remaining entrails.

B. Peel off the thin mottled skin and discard. Wash squid under cold running water. (If tentacles are large enough to bother with, skin as for body and cut into short lengths.)

Preparing mussels

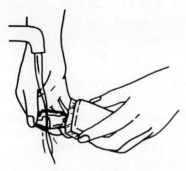

A. Scrub the shells thoroughly under cold running water using a stiff brush or scouring pad. Discard damaged ones or any that do not close when tapped on the edge of the sink.

B. Pull away any 'seaweed-like' beard.

C. Scrape off any barnacles with a knife.

Small clams and cockles are cleaned and sorted in the same way, although they tend to need less 'scrubbing'.

Venus clams usually only require a rinse after sifting through.

Preparing scallops

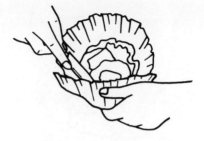

A. Using a rigid knife lever the shells apart. Cut the scallops from the rounded shell by sliding a knife between flesh and shell.

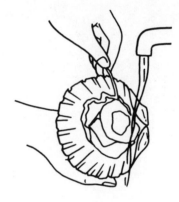

B. Rinse under cold water discarding the green or black intestine.

Preparing crab

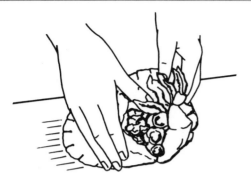

A. Twist off claws and legs. Push body away from shell.

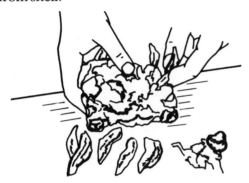

B. Pull away and discard soft feathery 'dead mens fingers'.

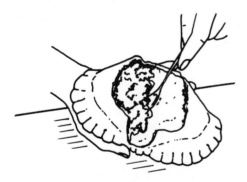

C. Cut body in half with a large knife and scrape out white meat from body and leg sockets using a skewer. Crack open claws with a hammer or rolling pin and scoop out flesh. If legs are large enough, crack and scoop out flesh in the same way, otherwise reserve for garnish. Scoop out soft brown meat from the shell. Discard stomach sac immediately behind crab's mouth. If using shell as a serving container break shell along visible line on underside to leave a neat rim. Scrub shell before using.

NOTES ON USING THE RECIPES

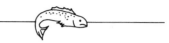

1.   Cooking times will vary slightly depending on the initial temperature of the fish. As most fish is bought and stored chilled I have used fish at refrigerator temperature. Reduce cooking time if your fish has been unrefrigerated.

2.   Frozen fish can be substituted for fresh in stews and soups without thawing first. Allow a little extra cooking time. Fish that is cooked without sauce or liquid is best thawed first, otherwise the edges will be cooked before the centre has defrosted.

3.   Those recipes marked with ★ are those which I consider suitable (even necessary at the price!) for entertaining.

4.   Unless stated otherwise, all recipes are covered with cling film, folded back at one edge before cooking.

5.   Follow either metric or imperial quantities for the recipes; they are not interchangeable.

6.   All the recipes in this book were tested in a 650 watt microwave, so add a little cooking time if your oven has a lower wattage, and decrease cooking time if it has a higher wattage. Unless otherwise stated, all cooking times given are HIGH.

STOCKS
AND
SAUCES

FISH FUMET

This rich fish stock gives far better results than the bought 'cube' but takes little more effort to prepare. Use skins, bones, heads, tails – the lot – for maximum flavour. Crab and prawn shells can also be used to give delicious results for shellfish dishes.

Makes 900 ml (1½ pints)

1 onion, peeled and quartered
1 carrot, peeled and sliced
1 stick of celery, sliced
450 g (1 lb) fish trimmings
15 black peppercorns
5 ml (1 tsp) wine vinegar

1. Place onion, carrot and celery in a bowl with the fish trimmings, peppercorns, wine vinegar and 900 ml (1½ pints) water.

2. Cover and microwave on HIGH for 10 minutes, stirring once. Leave to cool then strain through a sieve.

COURT BOUILLON

Because the microwave cooks fish in its own moisture without drying it out, the need for this classic poaching liquid is virtually eliminated. However, it is still useful as a flavoured liquid for fish soups, emitting the delicate flavours of vegetables and herbs.

Makes about 600 ml (1 pint)

1 carrot, roughly chopped
1 small leek, sliced
1 stick of celery, roughly chopped
150 ml (¼ pint) dry white wine
20 black peppercorns, crushed
1 bouquet garni sachet
2 bay leaves

1. Place the vegetables in a bowl. Cover and microwave on HIGH for 2 minutes.

2. Add the wine, peppercorns, bouquet garni, bay leaves and 450 ml (15 fl oz) water.

3. Cover and microwave on HIGH for 10 minutes, stirring once. Leave to cool then strain.

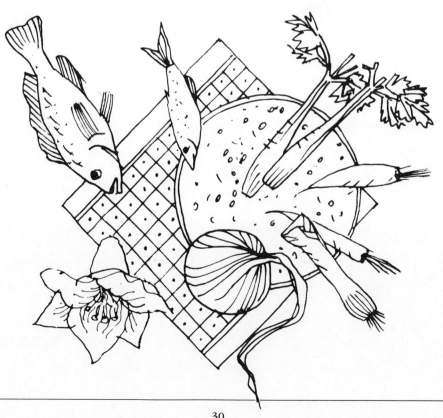

BECHAMEL SAUCE

Used as an integral part of a recipe or as an interesting accompaniment, this smooth velvety sauce is without doubt the most useful you can make. Variations are listed below but it is equally adaptable to any other exciting flavourings of your own choice. They can all be further enhanced with a dash of cream before serving.

Makes about 300 ml (½ pint)

25 g (1 oz) butter or margarine
30 ml (2 level tbsp) plain flour
300 ml (½ pint) milk
salt and freshly ground black pepper

1. Place the butter in a 1.2 litre (2 pint) bowl. Microwave on HIGH for 1 minute until melted.

2. Stir in the flour and microwave on HIGH for 40 seconds.

3. Gradually whisk in the milk and microwave on HIGH for a further 2–3 minutes, whisking several times, until the sauce is thickened and smooth. Season to taste.

——— VARIATION ———

Mushroom: Finely chop 175 g (6 oz) mushrooms. Place in the bowl while melting the butter and microwave on HIGH for 3 minutes. Continue as above.

Cheese: Finely chop or grate 50 g (2 oz) mature Cheddar cheese and whisk into the sauce after thickening. Reheat for 1 minute, then season to taste.

Blue Brie: Chop 100 g (4 oz) blue brie, discarding rind. Add to the sauce after thickening. Reheat for 1 minute, then season to taste.

Parsley: Beat 60 ml (4 level tbsp) chopped parsley into the finished sauce.

Mustard: Beat 30 ml (2 level tbsp) coarse grain mustard and a good pinch of caster sugar into the finished sauce.

Anchovy: Drain the fillets from a 50 g (2 oz) can of anchovies. Blend with the milk until smooth, then continue as above.

HOLLANDAISE SAUCE

Whether spooned over seafood salads, poached salmon or fish mousses, Hollandaise sauce adds that 'special occasion' flavour. Like the conventionally prepared version it must be served immediately so measure out ingredients, ready for last minute cooking.

Serves 4–6

100 g (4 oz) butter
3 egg yolks
30 ml (2 tbsp) lemon juice
salt and white pepper

1. Place the butter in a large bowl. Microwave on HIGH for 2–3 minutes until melted.

2. Add the egg yolks and lemon juice and beat with an electric whisk until frothy.

3. Microwave on HIGH for 30 seconds. Whisk again. Microwave for a further 30 seconds, whisk until very thick and creamy.

4. Season to taste and serve immediately.

WATERCRESS SAUCE

Beautifully smooth and colourful, a creamy watercress sauce, used in moderation, makes a stylish accompaniment to seafood mousses and most 'dry cooked' fish, particularly salmon. Blanching the leaves in boiling water is not essential but removes the 'harshness' often associated with watercress.

Makes about 300 ml ($\frac{1}{2}$ pint)

75 g (3 oz) watercress
knob of butter
$\frac{1}{2}$ small onion, peeled and chopped
150 ml ($\frac{1}{4}$ pint) fish or vegetable stock or fish fumet
150 ml ($\frac{1}{4}$ pint) single cream
salt and freshly ground black pepper

1. Remove any tough stalks from the watercress. Place watercress in a bowl of boiling water and leave for 1 minute. Drain thoroughly.

2. Place the butter in a bowl and microwave on HIGH for 30 seconds until melted. Add onion, cover and microwave for 1 minute.

3. Add watercress and stock and blend mixture in a liquidizer or food processor until smooth.

4. Return to the bowl with the cream and seasoning and microwave on MEDIUM for 1 minute until heated through, stirring once.

RICH TOMATO SAUCE

For tossing with pasta or accompanying richer fish dishes, a highly flavoured tomato sauce makes an indispensible standby. Unless you have a glut supply of fresh tomatoes use canned, the flavour is equally good and colour always richer.

Makes 600 ml (1 pint)

15 ml (1 tbsp) olive oil
1 onion, peeled and chopped
1 garlic clove, skinned and crushed (optional)
1 stick of celery, sliced
400 g (14 oz) can chopped tomatoes
1.5 ml ($\frac{1}{4}$ level tsp) caster sugar
30 ml (2 level tbsp) tomato purée
5 ml (1 level tsp) fresh chopped oregano or basil or 2.5 ml ($\frac{1}{2}$ level tsp) dried
salt and freshly ground black pepper

1. Place oil in a dish with the onion, garlic, and celery. Cover and microwave on HIGH for 3 minutes stirring once.

2. Add tomatoes, sugar, tomato purée, herbs and seasoning. Cover and microwave on HIGH for a further 5 minutes until pulpy, stirring once.

—— VARIATION ——
Fresh tomato sauce: Place 700 g (1$\frac{1}{2}$ lb) fresh tomatoes in a bowl. Cover with boiling water and leave for 1 minute. Drain and peel off skins. Add to sauce in place of canned tomatoes, breaking up with a wooden spoon as they soften. Add extra tomato purée to improve colour.

RED WINE SAUCE

Unusual with fish but fashionable! Use to add colour to 'peaky' looking dishes.

Makes about 300 ml (½ pint)

4 shallots, peeled and roughly chopped
1 rasher of streaky bacon, chopped
1 carrot, peeled and thinly sliced
300 ml (½ pint) red wine
15 ml (1 level tbsp) tomato purée
salt and freshly ground black pepper
1 bay leaf
15 g (½ oz) butter, softened
15 ml (1 level tbsp) plain flour

1. Place the shallots in a bowl with the bacon and carrot. Cover and microwave on HIGH for 2 minutes, stirring once until the carrots have softened.

2. Add the wine, tomato purée, seasoning and bay leaf. Cover and microwave on HIGH for 10 minutes, stirring once. Remove bay leaf.

3. Blend the mixture in a liquidizer or food processor then press through a sieve into a clean bowl.

4. Beat the butter and flour to a smooth paste. Whisk into the sauce. Microwave on HIGH for 2 minutes, stirring frequently until thickened and smooth. Season to taste.

WHITE WINE SAUCE

Muscadet, Chablis, Sancerre and any other dry white wines associated with fish will give good results in this recipe – a thrifty way of using up leftovers from an opened bottle. Use to enliven servings of white or oily fish.

Serves 4

25 g (1 oz) butter
2 shallots, peeled and finely chopped
15 ml (1 level tbsp) plain flour
250 ml (8 fl oz) dry white wine
2.5 ml (½ level tsp) finely chopped fresh parsley, chevil or tarragon
salt and freshly ground black pepper
30 ml (2 tbsp) single cream

1. Place the butter in a bowl and microwave on HIGH for 1 minute until melted. Add shallots and microwave on HIGH for 2 minutes, stirring once.

2. Add the flour and microwave on HIGH for 30 seconds. Gradually whisk in wine, herbs and seasoning. Cover and microwave on HIGH for 2 minutes, whisking twice, until thickened.

3. Stir in cream before serving.

CREAM CHEESE AND CHIVE SAUCE

Better suited to serving warm rather than hot, this simple sauce should be watched closely in the microwave as the cooking time will depend on the initial temperature of the cream cheese. Dried chives can be substituted if necessary, but make well ahead to let the flavour re-emerge.

Serves 4

100 g (4 oz) cream cheese
90 ml (6 tbsp) milk
10–15 ml (2–3 level tsp) creamed horseradish
30 ml (2 level tbsp) chopped chives
salt and freshly ground black pepper

1. Place the cream cheese in a bowl and beat with a balloon or electric whisk until softened.

2. Gradually beat in the milk, horseradish and chives until smooth.

3. Microwave on MEDIUM for 45 seconds to 1 minute until warmed through, stirring once. Season to taste.

——— SERVING SUGGESTION ———
Use in moderation to dress up white fish fillets, steaks and salmon. Any leftovers make a pleasant dipping sauce for prawns.

SABAYON SAUCE

A very light herb sauce that will add colour to any delicately flavoured fish. Have the herb infusion, and egg yolks ready – the whisking can be quickly performed between courses.

Serves 6

2 bay leaves
1 stick of celery, chopped
1 sprig of fresh rosemary or thyme
15 ml (1 level tbsp) fresh chopped parsley
3 egg yolks
5 ml (1 tsp) lemon juice
salt and freshly ground black pepper
15 g ($\frac{1}{2}$ oz) butter

1. Place the bay leaves, celery and rosemary or thyme in a small bowl. Add 75 ml (5 tbsp) boiling water and microwave on HIGH for 1 minute. Leave to cool slightly then strain.

2. Place the parsley, egg yolks, lemon juice and a little seasoning in a separate bowl. Microwave on HIGH for about 20 seconds until just warmed through.

3. Whisk with an electric beater until thickened and pale.

4. Gradually whisk the herb infusion into the yolks until foamy. Microwave on HIGH for a further 30 seconds.

5. Add the butter, cut into small pieces and whisk lightly before serving.

SWEET AND SOUR SAUCE

A piquant sauce that lacks the over thickened, gloopy consistency of many sauces of this nature. Use to add zip to shellfish cocktails, seafood brochettes or white fish fillets and steaks.

Serves 4–6

2.5 cm (1 in) piece fresh root ginger
1 small onion, peeled and finely chopped
1 garlic clove, skinned and crushed
15 ml (1 tbsp) oil
grated zest and juice of 1 orange
30 ml (2 tbsp) red or white wine vinegar
5 ml (1 level tsp) coarse grain mustard
30 ml (2 tbsp) medium sweet sherry
5 ml (1 tsp) black treacle
5 ml (1 level tsp) tomato purée
2.5 ml ($\frac{1}{2}$ level tsp) cornflour
salt and freshly ground black pepper

1. Peel the ginger and finely chop. Place in a bowl with the onion, garlic and oil. Cover and microwave on HIGH for 3 minutes, stirring twice until softened.

2. Stir in the orange zest and juice, vinegar, mustard, sherry, treacle and tomato purée. Cover and microwave on HIGH for 3 minutes, stirring once.

3. Blend the cornflour with 15 ml (1 tbsp) water. Add to bowl, cover and microwave on HIGH for a further 1 minute until thickened. Season to taste.

--- SERVING SUGGESTION ---

As only small quantities of this recipe are required per portion, keep remainder in a screw-topped jar, in the refrigerator, for up to 1 week.

PINK SEAFOOD SAUCE

Next time the family has whole prawns keep the trimmings for the basis of this rich sauce which gives a little 'lift' to any plain poached white fish. If there are not enough trimmings at one meal save them up in the freezer.

Makes 600 ml (1 pint)

trimmings from 450 g (1 lb) whole prawns
2.5 ml ($\frac{1}{2}$ level tsp) cornflour
15 ml (1 level tbsp) tomato purée
5 ml (1 tsp) white wine vinegar
2.5 ml ($\frac{1}{2}$ level tsp) caster sugar
150 ml ($\frac{1}{4}$ pint) Greek strained yogurt
salt and freshly ground black pepper

1. Place the prawn shells in a bowl with 600 ml (1 pint) water. Cover and microwave on HIGH for 10 minutes, stirring once.

2. Blend in a food processor or liquidizer and reserve.

3. Blend cornflour with 15 ml (1 tbsp) water in a bowl. Press prawn mixture through a sieve into the bowl.

4. Stir in tomato purée, vinegar, sugar, yogurt and a little seasoning. Microwave on MEDIUM for 2 minutes or until warmed through and slightly thickened, whisking twice.

SOUPS
AND
STARTERS

FRIDAY SOUP

A recipe for traditionalists who enjoy the classic combination of white fish, parsley sauce and boiled potatoes. This easy soup version is ideal for frozen 'blocks' of cod or haddock, as there is no need to search for bones.

Serves 4

1 onion, peeled and roughly chopped
1 stick of celery, roughly sliced
10 ml (2 tsp) oil
1 medium potato, peeled and roughly chopped
450 ml (15 fl oz) milk
pinch of nutmeg
small handful of parsley
salt and freshly ground black pepper
225 g (8 oz) cod or haddock, skinned and boned
50 g (2 oz) peas

1. Place the onion, celery and oil in a large bowl. Cover and microwave on HIGH for 3 minutes, stirring once.

2. Stir in the potato. Cover and microwave on HIGH for 3 minutes until the potato has softened.

3. Add the milk, nutmeg, parsley and seasoning and blend in a liquidizer or food processor until smooth. Return to the bowl and add the fish and peas.

4. Cover and microwave on HIGH for 4 minutes, until fish flakes easily, stirring twice. Season to taste before serving.

——— COOK'S TIP ———
If using frozen fish there is no need to thaw first. Add the fish to the pureed mixture and microwave on HIGH for 3 minutes before adding the peas.

SPICED COLEY CHOWDER

Cooked with Indian-style spices the slightly coarse flavour of coley is perfectly disguised to make an extremely cheap but delicious soup. Quantities are large, but the cooled soup freezes well.

Serves 6–8

1 onion, peeled and chopped
10 ml (2 tsp) oil
1.5 ml ($\frac{1}{4}$ level tsp) each of ground turmeric, cumin and coriander
2.5 ml ($\frac{1}{2}$ level tsp) fennel seeds
700 g (1$\frac{1}{2}$ lb) coley fillet
600 ml (1 pint) milk
350 g (12 oz) potatoes, peeled and diced
$\frac{1}{2}$ × 225 g (8 oz) carton Greek strained yogurt

1. Place onion in a large bowl with the oil, turmeric, cumin, coriander and fennel seeds. Cover and microwave on HIGH for 3 minutes.

2. Place fish in a dish with 30 ml (2 tbsp) of the milk. Cover and microwave on HIGH for 3 minutes.

3. Drain fish, adding liquid to onion mixture. Flake fish and add to bowl with the potatoes, remaining milk and seasoning.

4. Cover and microwave on HIGH for 15 minutes until potatoes are tender.

5. Stir in yogurt and heat through on MEDIUM for a further 2 minutes.

WUN TUN SOUP

Court Bouillon forms the base of this oriental soup, finished with finely cut vegetables and miniature dumplings concealing a prawn paste. If you live near an Oriental supermarket use their ready made 'wun tun wrappers' in place of the dumpling dough to speed preparation.

Serves 4

Dumplings

100 g (4 oz) plain flour
pinch of salt
1 egg yolk
225 g (8 oz) whole prawns
5 ml (1 tsp) soy sauce

Soup

5 ml (1 tsp) sesame or vegetable oil
1 carrot, cut into matchstick-sized shreds
1 bunch spring onions, trimmed and sliced diagonally
50 g (2 oz) spring greens, shredded
600 ml (1 pint) Court Bouillon (see page 30)
10 ml (2 tsp) soy sauce
5 ml (1 level tsp) caster sugar
salt and freshly ground black pepper

1. Sift the flour and salt into a bowl. Add egg yolk and 45 ml (3 tbsp) water. Mix to a firm dough, adding a little more water if necessary. Chill dough for 30 minutes. Peel 8 of the prawns, leaving tails on and reserve.

2. Peel remainder. Roughly chop and then beat to a paste with the soy sauce.

3. Roll out the dough as thinly as possible on a lightly floured surface. Cut into 4 cm (1½ in) squares. Brush edges of squares with water and spoon a little prawn mixture into the centre of each. Bring edges of parcels up over filling and press together with fingers to form little bundles.

4. Place the oil, carrot, spring onions and spring greens in a large bowl. Cover and microwave on HIGH for 2 minutes, stirring once.

5. Add the Court Bouillon, soy sauce, sugar, seasoning and 200 ml (7 fl oz) water. Cover and microwave on HIGH for 2 minutes until heated through.

6. Add reserved prawns and dumplings. Cover and microwave on HIGH for a further 4 minutes until dumplings are tender. Leave to stand for 2 minutes.

—— COOK'S TIP ——

For good results it is important to roll the dough as thinly as possible. If too thick the dumplings will remain doughy and undercooked in the centres.

See photograph page 41

SEAFOOD BISQUE

★ *A bisque is a rich, creamy fish soup that should, with the careful addition of Tabasco or cayenne, have a faint 'hotness' about it. A richly flavoured stock is the key to success, so make good use of the crab and prawn shells to flavour the fumet.*

Serves 6

450 g (1 lb) crab, whole or claws
225 g (8 oz) whole prawns
900 ml (1½ pints) Fish Fumet (see page 30)
2 shallots, peeled and chopped
30 ml (2 tbsp) olive oil
25 g (1 oz) plain flour
5 ml (1 level tsp) lemon rind, grated
10 ml (2 tsp) brandy
1.5 ml (¼ level tsp) ground mace
30 ml (2 level tbsp) tomato purée
150 ml (¼ pint) double cream
few drops Tabasco or good pinch cayenne pepper
salt and freshly ground black pepper

1. Remove meat from crab and reserve. Shell prawns. Make fish fumet using shells from prawns and crab.

2. Place shallots in a bowl with the oil. Cover and microwave on HIGH for 1½ minutes. Add flour and microwave for 1 minute.

3. Gradually blend in stock then lemon rind, brandy, mace and tomato purée. Cover and microwave on HIGH for 7 minutes, whisking twice, until slightly thickened.

4. Add crab and prawn meat and blend in a liquidizer or food processor until smooth. Return to bowl.

5. Stir in cream, Tabasco and seasoning to taste. Cover and microwave on HIGH for 2 minutes or until heated through.

—— COOK'S TIP ——

You can get maximum value from a lobster by using the leftover shell and legs in place of the crab. If you are sufficiently organised reserve a few morsels of the lobster flesh and use to garnish the bisque.

WALNUT FUMET SOUP

★ *This delicately creamy soup shows just how flavoursome a good fish stock can be in a recipe without the addition of extra fish! Here it is blended with nuts and garlic for a mouth-watering dinner party starter.*

Serves 6

1 garlic clove, skinned and roughly chopped
75 g (3 oz) walnuts
75 g (3 oz) blanched almonds
900 ml–1.2 litres (1½–2 pints) Fish Fumet (see page 30)
salt and freshly ground black pepper
60 ml (4 tbsp) single cream

Garnish

croûtons
snipped chives

1. Place the garlic in a liquidizer or food processor with the walnuts, almonds and 150 ml (¼ pint) of the stock. Blend until smooth.

2. Add another 150 ml (¼ pint) of the stock and blend further. Press through a sieve into a large bowl.

3. Stir in the remaining stock and seasoning. Cover and microwave on HIGH for 3 minutes or until heated through. Stir in the cream.

4. Divide among soup bowls and garnish with croûtons and chives.

CLAM CHOWDER

This American speciality is one of many versions of the thick and chunky potato enriched soups collectively called 'chowders'. This recipe is designed as a starter (if quantities are kept small) although heaftier portions would make a nourishing meal if served with plenty of bread. For a smoother result purée soup rather than mash.

Serves 6–8

12 large clams, scrubbed
1 onion, peeled and chopped
100 g (4 oz) salt pork, finely diced
15 ml (1 tbsp) oil
300 ml ($\frac{1}{2}$ pint) tomato juice
350 g (12 oz) potatoes, peeled and diced
2.5 ml ($\frac{1}{2}$ level tsp) fresh chopped thyme or 1.5 ml ($\frac{1}{4}$ level tsp) dried
2.5 ml ($\frac{1}{2}$ level tsp) ground paprika or few drops Tabasco sauce
30 ml (2 tbsp) double cream

1. Place clams in a large bowl. Cover and microwave on HIGH for 8–10 minutes until opened. Discard any which remain closed. Reserve cooking juices. Remove clams from shells and finely chop (if difficult to remove from shells microwave for a little longer). Make clam juices up to 450 ml (15 fl oz) with water and reserve.

2. Place onion and pork in a bowl with the oil and microwave on HIGH for 3 minutes, stirring once.

3. Add clams and tomato juice, potatoes, thyme and paprika or Tabasco. Cover and microwave on HIGH for 12–15 minutes, stirring twice until potatoes are tender.

4. Mash chowder with a potato masher until potatoes are slightly broken up. Add the cream and return to microwave for 1 minute until reheated.

—— COOK'S TIP ——

Caution is needed when seasoning the 'chowder'. Clams are naturally very salted so wait until preparation is finished before adjusting the seasoning.

From left to right: Wun tun soup (page 38); Prawn patia (page 48) and Fish biyildi (page 80).

OVERLEAF

From the left clockwise: Family fish stew (page 98); Baked mackerel with foaming orange sauce (page 95); Fennel salad with Bel Paese dressing (page 122); Swordfish pâté (page 49) and Pink salmon salad (page 52).

A selection of seafood with Delicate cheese fondue (page 94) and Warm spinach salad (page 121).

SUMMER ROE AND CUCUMBER SOUP

★ *Try this recipe on anyone who insists that they could not possibly indulge in 'cold fish soup'. Blended with cucumber and yogurt, cheap and cheerful herring roes make a starter worthy of the most splendid gathering.*

Serves 6–8

450 g (1 lb) soft herring roe
15 g (½ oz) butter
½ cucumber, roughly sliced
350 ml (12 fl oz) Court Bouillon (see page 30)
150 ml (¼ pint) natural yogurt
45 ml (3 level tbsp) mayonnaise
salt and freshly ground black pepper

Garnish

croûtons

diced cucumber

1.   Cut the herring roes into small pieces.

2.   Place the butter in a bowl and microwave on HIGH for 1 minute until melted. Add the roes and the cucumber, cover and microwave on HIGH for 5 minutes, stirring once, until the roes are cooked through.

3.   Place in a liquidizer or food processor and blend until smooth. Return to bowl and stir in the Court Bouillon, yogurt, mayonnaise and seasoning. Chill the soup thoroughly until ready to serve.

4.   Serve in soup bowls garnished with croûtons and diced cucumber.

RICH SEAFOOD SOUP

★ *This, my favourite fish soup of all, is made by throwing whole, choice fresh fish into a pot, cooking briefly, puréeing and pressing vigorously through a sieve to extract every morsel of flavour and goodness. It defies any suggestion that these French-style soups are difficult to make, although plenty of time must be allowed for the sieving. I serve it with a bowl of hot garlicky Rouille, plenty of warmed bread and chilled white wine, for a magnificent and hearty starter.*

Serves 6

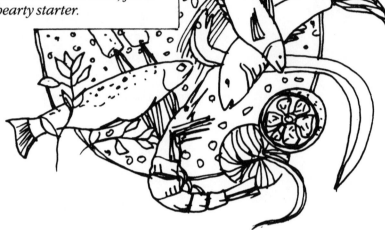

45 ml (3 tbsp) olive oil
1 onion, peeled and chopped
1 garlic clove, skinned and crushed
1 carrot, peeled and chopped
45 ml (3 level tbsp) long grain rice
900 g (2 lb) mixed fish (eg gurnard, mullet, conger eel, John Dory, whole prawns, cod or haddock), gutted and cut into pieces if large
grated zest of 1 lemon
2.5 ml (½ level tsp) lightly crushed saffron strands, soaked overnight in 30 ml (2 tbsp) boiling water
1.5 ml (1 level tbsp) tomato puree
salt and freshly ground black pepper

To serve

1 quantity Rouille (see page 123)

1. Place the oil in a large bowl with the onion, garlic and carrots. Cover and microwave on HIGH for 5 minutes until softened, stirring once.

2. Stir in the rice, fish, lemon zest and saffron. Pour over 1.45 litres (2½ pints) of boiling water.

3. Cover and microwave on HIGH for 10 minutes, stirring twice.

4. Leave mixture to cool slightly then place, in small batches, in a liquidizer or food processor. Blend until smooth.

5. Press the mixture through a sieve into a clean bowl. (The sieve will be virtually full of debris at the end.)

6. Stir the tomato puree into the soup and microwave on HIGH for about 3 minutes until heated through. Season to taste.

7. Ladle the soup into large bowls and serve with the Rouille, for guests to stir into their soup.

OYSTER STEW

★ *People seem to love or hate oysters. I lack the appreciation for the raw delicacy, swallowed whole with a dash of Tabasco, but enjoy this incredibly simple stew. You need only allow three oysters per serving but choose your smallest serving containers so that the portions do not look mean.*

Serves 4

12 oysters

15 g ($\frac{1}{2}$ oz) butter

150 ml ($\frac{1}{4}$ pint) single cream

few drops Tabasco sauce

pinch of salt

pinch of paprika

To serve

buttered wholemeal toast

1. To open an oyster, insert a sturdy knife between the shells, next to the hinged end. Twist the knife and push against the hinge until it breaks open, working over a bowl to catch the juices. Open out the shells and cut through the muscle attached to the rounded shell. Run a knife under the oyster to free it from the flat shell. Repeat with the remaining oysters.

2. Place the butter in a shallow dish and microwave on HIGH for 1 minute until melted. Add the oyster juices, cream and a dash of Tabasco. Cover and microwave on MEDIUM for 1 minute or until heated through.

3. Add the oysters and microwave on MEDIUM for 1½–2 minutes until just heated through and beginning to 'shrink' slightly.

4. Season with salt if necessary and divide among serving dishes. Sprinkle with paprika and serve with wholemeal toast.

—— SERVING SUGGESTION ——
The rounded oyster shells make visually appealing serving containers. Rinse out and then plunge into boiling water for 5 minutes. After drying, arrange three on each serving plate ready for the stew to be spooned in.

SPECIAL SEAFOOD STEW

★ *Fish stews need not be limited to main courses. Small quantities make appetising starters, particularly if you include expensive fish that you might not be able to afford as a main course. This recipe, using scallops, prawns and monkfish with a hint of aniseed, is enchanced by using scallop shells as serving dishes.*

Serves 6

$\frac{1}{2}$ small fennel bulb

100 g (4 oz) monkfish

225 g (8 oz) scallops

10 ml (2 tsp) olive oil

3 spring onions, trimmed and sliced

1 stick of celery, sliced

400 g (14 oz) can plum tomatoes

2.5 ml ($\frac{1}{2}$ level tsp) caster sugar

30 ml (2 tbsp) Pernod

salt and freshly ground black pepper

100 g (4 oz) peeled prawns

Garnish

sprigs of fennel

1. Thinly slice fennel, discarding central core.

2. Cut monkfish into small cubes. Halve or quarter scallops (depending on size).

3. Place oil, onions, celery and fennel in a dish. Cover and microwave on HIGH for 4 minutes, stirring once. Add scallops and monkfish and cook for 2 minutes.

4. Stir in the tomatoes from the can, sugar, Pernod, seasoning and prawns. Divide among 6 scallop shells or ramekins.

5. Cover and microwave on HIGH for 1–2 minutes until heated through.

6. Garnish each with a sprig of fennel and serve.

PRAWN PATIA

★ *A pretty 'hot' starter for four (or indulgent treat for two) that requires a richly flavoured main course. So if serving fish to follow avoid expensive, subtle flavours like sole or salmon.*

Serves 4

6 popadoms
15 ml (1 tbsp) olive oil
1 small onion, peeled and chopped
1.5 ml (¼ level tsp) ground turmeric
2.5 ml (½ level tsp) each ground cumin and mild chilli powder
450 g (1 lb) whole prawns, peeled, or 100–175 g (4–6 oz) ready peeled prawns
2.5 ml (½ level tsp) fresh chopped coriander
227 g (8 oz) can chopped tomatoes
15 ml (1 tbsp) white wine or garlic vinegar
5 ml (1 tsp) caster sugar
salt and freshly ground black pepper

Garnish

open leaf parsley or coriander

1. Brush one side of each popadom with oil. Cook, one at a time for 30–45 seconds until puffed up. Drain on kitchen paper.

2. Place remaining oil in a dish with the onion and spices. Cover and microwave on HIGH for 4 minutes until softened, stirring once.

3. Add prawns, coriander, tomatoes, vinegar, sugar and seasoning and microwave on HIGH for a further 2 minutes.

4. Spoon mixture over popadoms and serve garnished with parsley or coriander.

See photograph page 41

BAKED GIANT PRAWNS WITH GARLIC DRESSING

★ *The tastiest dishes are often the simplest, which is certainly the case with this starter, based on a conventionally baked recipe which uses only olive oil in the marinade. In adapting it to suit the microwave I have used a dressing instead – and the result is even better!*

Serves 6

12 giant prawns or 225 g (8 oz) ordinary prawns
3 small chillies, fresh or dried
6 garlic cloves, skinned
125 ml (4 fl oz) olive oil
45 ml (3 tbsp) white wine vinegar
salt

1. Arrange prawns on 6 small serving dishes.

2. Halve chillies. Pierce garlic with a knife. Place a chilli and clove of garlic into each dish.

3. Mix together oil, vinegar and a little salt and pour over the prawns.

4. Cover loosely and leave to marinade for 2 hours. Uncover dishes and space, slightly apart in the microwave. Cook on HIGH for 2–3 minutes until warmed through. (If plates are large you may need to cook 3 at a time).

—— SERVING SUGGESTION ——
Supply finger bowls and plenty of warmed bread for mopping up the delicious juices. The garlic can be eaten but only those with asbestos throats should tackle the chillies!

See photograph page 103

SWORDFISH PÂTÉ

★ *The firm meaty texture of swordfish makes it one of the best fish to serve 'pâté style'. As rich as most meat pâtés, it is best sliced as thinly as possible, giving ample portions and plenty left for a cold snack the following day.*

Serves 8

packet aspic jelly powder
150 ml (¼ pint) dry white wine
1 orange
open leaf parsley
450 g (1 lb) swordfish
salt and freshly ground black pepper
225 g (8 oz) cream cheese
10 ml (2 level tsp) powdered gelatine
227 g (8 oz) packet frozen chopped spinach

To serve

toast or crusty bread

1. Make up aspic jelly powder following manufacturer's instructions, substituting 150 ml (¼ pint) wine for an equal quantity of water. Leave to cool. Pour 75 ml (3 fl oz) into the base of a dampened 900 g (2 lb) loaf tin. Thinly pare a little rind from orange and cut out small petal shapes. Arrange, over aspic in a decorative pattern with the parsley. Chill until firm, then pour over a further 75 ml (3 fl oz) of aspic.

2. Place swordfish on a plate. Season lightly. Cover and microwave on HIGH for 5 minutes until cooked through, re-arranging fish once.

3. Roughly flake fish into a liquidizer or food processor discarding skin and bone. Grate remaining orange rind and add to swordfish with the cream cheese and all but 125 ml (4 fl oz) of the aspic. Blend until smooth.

4. Sprinkle gelatine over 150 ml (¼ pint) boiling water until dissolved. Beat into swordfish mixture.

5. Prick bag of spinach and microwave on HIGH for 3–4 minutes until heated through. Press in a sieve to squeeze out excess water. Season spinach and mix with reserved aspic jelly.

6. Spoon half the swordfish mixture over aspic in base of loaf tin and level surface. Chill for a few minutes until firm. Spoon spinach mixture over swordfish and level surface. Cover with remaining swordfish mixture and chill until completely firm, about 4 hours.

7. To serve pâté: dip loaf tin in boiling water for 5–10 seconds then turn out onto a serving plate. Serve cut into slices.

—— COOK'S TIP ——
Shark makes an equally successful alternative, but if neither are available use a firm textured white fish. The result will be good, although texture not as firm.

See photograph page 43

WARM SEAFOOD SALAD

★ *Once you have gathered your choice of exotica for this stylish salad, there is little more to do than heat it through in the microwave. If your pocket can stretch to it, buy raw prawns and cook them in the butter before adding the remaining fish. They are ready as soon as they turn deep pink.*

Serves 6

Dressing

60 ml (4 tbsp) olive oil

15 ml (1 tbsp) white wine vinegar

1 garlic clove, skinned and crushed (optional)

salt and freshly ground black pepper

½ crisp lettuce, preferably oakleaf or curley endive

25 g (1 oz) butter

10 ml (2 level tsp) pesto

6 king prawns

300 ml (½ pint) whole prawns

300 ml (½ pint) mussels, scrubbed

1. Mix together the oil, vinegar, garlic and seasoning. Break the lettuce into manageable pieces and toss in the dressing. Arrange on 6 serving plates.

2. Place the butter in a large shallow container with the pesto and a little seasoning. Microwave on HIGH for 1 minute until the butter has melted.

3. Add the king prawns and toss in the butter mixture. Cover and microwave on HIGH for 30 seconds. Stir in the whole prawns and mussels. Cover and microwave on HIGH for a further 3 minutes until heated through and mussels have opened.

4. Arrange the fish attractively over the salad, reserving any unopened mussels. Return these to the microwave and cook for a further 1 minute. Add to the plates, discarding any mussels which still remain closed.

5. Serve the salad with fingerbowls.

——— COOK'S TIP ———
Pesto is an Italian sauce of basil, Parmesan and pine kernals, now widely available in jars at supermarkets and the delicatessen.

See photograph page 63

SMOKED COD ROE MOUSSE

★ *Smoked Cod Roe makes a deliciously smooth mousse that should appeal to all Taramasalata lovers, a dish for which it is invariably reserved. Fairly rich in flavour this mousse is best followed by something simple, perhaps a crisp bowl of salad or light pasta dish.*

Serves 6

175 g (6 oz) smoked cod roe
300 ml (½ pint) Bechamel sauce (see page 31)
2 eggs
150 ml (¼ pint) double cream

Garnish

sprigs of leaf parsley
pink lumpfish roe (optional)

To serve

Melba toast or crusty rolls

1. Remove the skin from the cod roe and cut roe into small pieces. Place in a food processor or liquidizer with the sauce and blend until smooth.

2. Separate eggs and beat yolks into the mixture with the cream. Whisk whites until peaking and fold in with a metal spoon.

3. Pour into 6 lightly oiled individual dishes. Cover each and arrange in a circle, spaced slightly apart in microwave. Cook on MEDIUM for about 4 minutes until surfaces feel just firm.

4. Leave to stand for 3 minutes then turn out onto small serving plates. Garnish with parsley and lumpfish roe, if liked. Serve with Melba toast or crusty rolls.

—— COOK'S TIP ——
Use microwave ramekin dishes or porcelain ones (without metallic rims). If neither are available use large teacups.

See cover photograph

STIR FRIED SQUID

A wonderfully easy starter that closely resembles Greek 'Mezze' style nibbles. Microwaved squid cooks in a flash, and is ready to eat as soon as it has puffed into the familiar 'rings'. Avoid overcooking which gives a rubbery texture.

Serves 4

450 g (1 lb) squid, cleaned
30 ml (2 tbsp) olive oil
1 garlic clove, skinned and crushed
strip of lemon rind, thinly pared
10 ml (2 tsp) lemon juice
12 stoned black olives
1 canned pimiento, drained and sliced
salt and freshly ground black pepper
15 ml (1 level tbsp) chopped parsley

To serve

toasted pitta bread

1. Cut the squid into rings and thoroughly dry on kitchen paper.

2. Preheat a browning dish, following manufacturer's directions.

3. Add the oil, garlic and squid and stir until sizzling dies down.

4. Add the lemon rind and juice, olives, pimiento and a little seasoning. Cover and microwave on HIGH for 1 minute.

5. Sprinkle with parsley and serve with pitta bread.

See photograph page 104

WARM KIPPER DIP

I often resist buying kippers because of the abundance of tiny bones, but this recipe whizzes them smooth in the blender. Once prepared the dip should be just warm, perfect for enjoying the smokey flavour. If left to go cold it firms up to a pâté consistency – harder to dip but equally tasty.

Serves 4–6

450 g (1 lb) kipper fillets
25 g (1 oz) butter
grated zest of 1 lemon
1 garlic clove, skinned and crushed
5 ml (1 level tsp) English mustard
150 ml (¼ pint) Greek strained yogurt

1. Place kipper fillets on a plate and dot with the butter. Cover and microwave on HIGH for 4 minutes, turning once. Discard skin and any bones.

2. Place the fish in a liquidizer or food processor with the lemon zest, garlic and mustard and blend until smooth.

3. Turn the mixture into a bowl and beat in the yogurt. Turn into a serving dish.

——— SERVING SUGGESTION ———
Surround dip with crûdité of crisp vegetables and breadsticks.

PINK SALMON SALAD

★ *Salmon and strawberries are most desirable in flavour and price at about the same time, a good reason for combining their fresh summer flavours in one luxurious starter. The crucial watchpoint is to microwave the salmon until it is barely cooked, to preserve its beautiful colour and texture.*

Serves 6

2 escalopes of salmon (about 450 g [1 lb] total weight)
1.5 ml (¼ level tsp) salt
2.5 ml (½ level tsp) fresh chopped dill or 1.5 ml (¼ level tsp) dried
15 ml (1 level tbsp) caster sugar
1 small red onion, peeled and cut into rings
90 ml (6 tbsp) red wine vinegar
freshly ground black pepper
175 g (6 oz) strawberries, halved if large

Garnish

sprigs of dill
red or black lumpfish roe

1. Remove skin and any bones from fish and lay fish, skinned side down in a shallow dish.

2. Mix together salt, dill and sugar and rub into surface of fish. Cut fish into narrow strips and lay in a single layer in dish. Leave to marinate for 30 minutes.

3. Cover dish and microwave on MEDIUM for 2½–3 minutes until fish is only just cooked, re-arranging once. Arrange onion rings over fish and pour over vinegar. Season to taste.

4. Divide among small serving plates with the strawberries. Keep in a cool place until needed.

5. Serve garnished with sprigs of dill and red or black lumpfish roe.

See photograph page 42

TRIO OF SMOKED FISH WITH MELON SAUCE

★ *A dinner party starter for adventurous diners! The intense richness of smoked fish needs a light, refreshing sauce like this mildly spiced melon purée. Choose from smoked eel, salmon, mackerel, halibut or kippers (the latter two will need lightly cooking first) and arrange small portions attractively on the dishes. An arrangement of three fish looks attractive but you can choose more or less, depending on availability.*

Serves 6

550 g (1¼ lb) mixture of smoked fish, lightly cooked if necessary
1 melon, about 450 g (1 lb)
5 cardamom pods
15 ml (1 tbsp) lemon juice
a little black pepper

To serve

buttered wholemeal bread

1. If using eel, cut into thin slices. Break mackerel, halibut or kipper into smaller pieces. If using smoked salmon, cut into thin strips. Arrange fish on 6 serving plates.

2. Remove the seeds from the melon and scoop about 18 small balls from the flesh using a melon baller.

3. Place the remaining flesh in a liquidizer or food processor. Open the cardamom pods and tip the seeds into the liquidizer with the lemon juice. Blend until smooth, then transfer to large measuring jug.

4. Cover and microwave on HIGH for 2 minutes until heated through. Season with pepper and add a little more lemon juice if necessary. (The sauce should be tangy but not sharp.)

5. Pour the sauce around the fish and serve with buttered wholemeal bread.

See photograph page 102

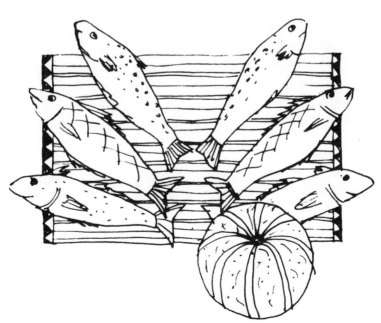

HERRING ROES WITH GREEN PEPPERCORN VINAIGRETTE

At my fishmongers, one thing I can always rely on buying – Monday or Friday – is herring roes. This is, I think because they keep a huge supply in the freezer. Despite this the roes taste good and make an interesting starter with a spicy flavoured dressing.

Serves 4

60 ml (4 tbsp) walnut or olive oil
15 ml (1 tbsp) garlic or white wine vinegar
10 ml (2 level tsp) green peppercorn purée
salt and freshly ground black pepper
350 g (12 oz) soft herring roes
25 g (1 oz) walnut pieces

1. Mix together 45 ml (3 tbsp) of the oil, the vinegar, peppercorn purée and seasoning.

2. Cut the herring roes into small pieces.

3. Preheat a browning dish following manufacturer's directions.

4. Add the remaining 15 ml (1 tbsp) of the oil and the roes and stir gently until the sizzling dies down. Cover and microwave on HIGH for 2½ minutes until cooked through, stirring once.

5. Drain the roes to warmed serving plates and spoon the dressing over. Sprinkle with walnut pieces.

HALIBUT AND BROCCOLI MOUSSE

★ *This combination of puréed halibut and broccoli makes an amazingly quick and deliciously light warm mousse. Once you have mastered the technique, experiment with other combinations of fish and vegetables and select a complimentary sauce, perhaps Watercress, Pink Seafood or Red or White Wine.*

Serves 6

100 g (4 oz) cream cheese
3 eggs
5 ml (1 tsp) lemon juice
1.5 ml (¼ level tsp) ground nutmeg
salt and freshly ground black pepper
350 g (12 oz) halibut
100 g (4 oz) frozen broccoli

1. Lightly grease a 1.2 litre (2 pint) pudding basin and line the base with greased greaseproof paper.

2. Place the cream cheese in a bowl and gradually whisk in the eggs until smooth. Beat in the lemon juice, nutmeg and seasoning.

3. Roughly chop the halibut, discarding skin and bones. Blend in a liquidizer or food processor with 30 ml (2 tbsp) water until smooth. Add to cream cheese mixture.

4. Place the broccoli in a dish with 30 ml (2 tbsp) water. Cover and microwave on HIGH for 2–3 minutes until defrosted. Blend until smooth then add to bowl.

5. Turn the mixture into prepared basin and cook, uncovered on MEDIUM for 10–12 minutes until firm. Leave to stand for 8 minutes.

6. Invert onto a plate and cut into wedges. Arrange on individual plates with a sauce spooned around.

— COOK'S TIP —
If substituting fresh broccoli, cut up any large stalks and arrange broccoli in a dish. Add 30 ml (2 tbsp) water. Cover and microwave on HIGH for 4–5 minutes until softened.

CREAM CHEESE AND PRAWN CROÛSTADES

★ *This pungent blend of cream cheese, garlic and prawns, spooned into crispy baked bread cases and served with a tangy fruit sauce makes an enticing dish for garlic lovers!*

Freshly peeled prawns are a 'must' for maximum flavour, so peel about 275 g (10 oz) to get the required amount of meat. Prepare the cases, filling and sauce a day in advance and assemble before dinner.

Serves 6

25 g (1 oz) butter
6 thin slices brown bread
100 g (4 oz) peeled prawns
1 garlic clove, skinned and crushed
75 g (3 oz) cream cheese
salt and freshly ground black pepper
225 g (8 oz) fresh or frozen redcurrants
2.5 ml (½ tsp) lemon juice
20 ml (4 level tsp) caster sugar

Garnish

6 whole prawns
extra redcurrants

1. Place the butter in a shallow dish and microwave on HIGH for 1 minute until melted.

2. Discard the crusts from bread to leave squares of about 7.5 cm (3 in). Lightly brush bread with the butter on both sides then press into sections of microwave tartlet cases.

3. Cover loosely with kitchen paper and microwave on HIGH for 5 minutes until the cases turn crisp. (They will crisp further while cooling.) Drain on kitchen paper.

4. Finely chop the prawns and beat in a bowl with the garlic, cream cheese and seasoning. Spoon mixture into the cooled bread cases.

5. Place the redcurrants in a bowl with the lemon juice, sugar and 30 ml (2 tbsp) water. Cover and microwave on HIGH for 3 minutes until fruit has softened. Press through a sieve into a small clean jug and microwave on HIGH for 30 seconds or until reheated.

6. Place the croûstades onto 6 serving plates and pour a little sauce around each.

7. Serve garnished with whole prawns and redcurrants.

—— COOK'S TIP ——

If you cannot get fresh or frozen redcurrants 'dress up' the contents of a small jar. Place in a bowl with 15 ml (1 tbsp) port or orange juice and microwave until melted.

See photograph page 62

SNACKS AND LIGHT MEALS FOR ONE AND TWO

SPICED SPRATS WITH CUCUMBER RAITA

The humble sprat should not be shunned for its meagreness, but snapped up for its sardine-like flavour. Arrange sunburst fashion around the yogurt dip, and serve with popadums or naan bread to continue the Indian theme.

Serves 2

15 g ($\frac{1}{2}$ oz) butter or margarine
450 g (1 lb) sprats, cleaned and gutted
10 ml (2 level tsp) plain flour
1.5 ml ($\frac{1}{4}$ level tsp) curry powder
salt and freshly ground black pepper
150 ml ($\frac{1}{4}$ pint) natural yogurt
5 cm (2 in) length cucumber, grated

1. Place the butter or margarine in a small bowl. Microwave on HIGH for 1 minute until melted. Use to lightly brush the fish.

2. Mix together the flour, curry powder and seasoning. Place in a sieve and dust a little over a large flat plate.

3. Arrange the fish in a sunburst on the plate leaving a hollow in the centre. Dust with the remaining flour mixture.

4. Cover loosely and microwave on HIGH for $2\frac{1}{2}$–3 minutes until cooked through. Leave to stand for 2 minutes.

5. Mix together the yogurt, cucumber and seasoning in a small serving bowl. Stand the bowl in the centre of the dish of sprats.

To serve one
Halve the above ingredients and microwave the sprats on HIGH for $1\frac{1}{2}$ minutes until cooked through.

MARINATED SARDINES

An unusual recipe in that the marinating takes place after the fish is cooked, rather than while still raw. Smelts, anchovies and sprats make excellent alternatives to the sardines, but fresh mint is indispensable.

Serves 1–2

450 g (1 lb) small sardines, gutted
75 ml (5 tbsp) olive oil
salt and freshly ground black pepper
10 ml (2 level tsp) fresh chopped mint
10 ml (2 tsp) garlic or wine vinegar
2 strips of pared lemon rind

1. Arrange the fish in a single layer in a shallow dish. Brush with a little of the oil and season with salt and pepper.

2. Cover and microwave on HIGH for 2 minutes until cooked through, re-arranging fish half way through cooking.

3. Mix together the remaining oil, mint, vinegar and seasoning and pour over the fish. Tuck the lemon rind around fish and keep in a cool place for at least 2 hours before serving.

—— COOK'S TIP ——
Gutting very small fish can be very time consuming. As a short cut remove head and then squeeze out intestines. Rinse under cold running water.

ONE POT NOODLES

A storecupboard version of the popular, but unfortunately 'junky' noodles available from the supermarkets. Throw all the ingredients in a bowl and refrigerate until lunchtime.

Serves 1

25 g (1 oz) egg noodles, broken into short lengths

227 g (8 oz) can chopped tomatoes

75 g (3 oz) can prawns in brine, drained

good pinch of curry powder

1.5 ml ($\frac{1}{4}$ level tsp) honey

25 g (1 oz) Cheddar cheese, grated

salt and freshly ground black pepper

1. Place all the ingredients in a serving bowl and refrigerate until required.

2. Cover and microwave on HIGH for 2 minutes, stirring once until pasta is tender.

3. Leave to stand for 2 minutes.

COCKLES WITH BLACK PEPPER

Just like mussels and clams, cockles are a sheer joy to cook in the microwave. Wide open shells are a sure sign that they are perfectly cooked, ready for dredging with vinegar and pepper. If liked, add a crushed clove of garlic before cooking.

Serves 2

1.2 litres (2 pints) cockles, cleaned

white wine vinegar

salt and freshly ground black pepper

To serve

brown bread or rolls and butter

1. Place the cockles in a large shallow dish. Cover and microwave on HIGH for 4 minutes until the shells have opened.

2. Return any shells that have not opened to the microwave for 2 minutes. Discard any that still remain closed.

3. Divide the cockles between 2 serving bowls and dredge with vinegar, black pepper and a little salt if liked. Serve with bread and butter.

To serve one
Use 600 ml (1 pint) of cockles and microwave on HIGH for 2–2$\frac{1}{2}$ minutes. Return any unopened shells to the microwave for a further 1 minute. Discard any that still remain closed.

FRESHLY POTTED PRAWNS

It is easy to tell when prawns are cooked. The flesh turns from a bluish grey to the more familiarly recognised pink colour. For flavour, these raw prawns are the best but ready cooked prawns can be substituted in this wonderfully simple but luxurious treat. Serve with a crispy salad, good bread and chilled white wine.

Serves 2

75 g (3 oz) unsalted butter
450 g (1 lb) whole prawns, raw or cooked
good pinch of ground mace
good pinch of cayenne pepper
salt

Garnish

parsley

1. If using uncooked prawns place 25 g (1 oz) of the butter in a large shallow dish. Microwave on HIGH for 1 minute until melted. Stir in the raw prawns. Cover and microwave on HIGH for 4 minutes, stirring twice until prawns have turned pink.

2. Shell the prawns and pack into 2 large ramekin dishes.

3. Place the remaining butter (or all the butter if using ready cooked prawns) in a dish. Microwave on HIGH for 3 minutes until the butter has melted and is just foaming but not beginning to brown.

4. Leave the butter for 30 seconds then clarify by pouring through a sieve, lined with a disposable kitchen cloth, into a clean bowl.

5. Season the clarified butter with the mace, cayenne pepper and salt then pour over the prawns.

6. Refrigerate until set, (ideally for 1 day to let the prawns flavour the butter).

7. Remove from the refrigerator 1 hour before serving. Turn the prawns out and serve with brown bread and butter.

To serve one
Halve the quantities of ingredients. Microwave the raw prawns for 2½ minutes, stirring once. Melt the butter for clarifying for 1½ to 2 minutes and continue as above.

—— **SERVING SUGGESTION** ——
Should you forget to remove the prawns from the refrigerator before serving, microwave on HIGH for 20 seconds to warm through slightly.

KEDGEREE

A traditional breakfast dish that is far more frequently served for lunch or supper. Fresh chopped coriander adds more interest than parsley but substitute a similar quantity of parsley if liked.

Serves 2

15 g (½ oz) butter or margarine
1 onion, peeled and chopped
100 g (4 oz) long grain rice
good pinch ground turmeric
300 ml (½ pint) fish stock, fish fumet or water
225 g (8 oz) smoked haddock, cod or whiting fillets
2 hard-boiled eggs, sliced
10 ml (2 level tsp) fresh chopped coriander
salt and freshly ground black pepper

1. Place butter or margarine in a shallow dish and microwave on HIGH for 1 minute until melted.

2. Add onion. Cover and microwave on HIGH for 3 minutes. Stir in rice, turmeric and fish stock or water. Cover and microwave on HIGH for 7 minutes.

3. Lay fish fillets over rice. Cover and microwave on HIGH for 2½–3 minutes until fish is cooked through.

4. Roughly flake fish and return to dish with the eggs, coriander and seasoning. Stir lightly and heat through for 1 minute. Leave to stand for 2 minutes before serving.

To serve one
Halve the ingredients above. Microwave the rice mixture for 4–5 minutes until almost tender. Add the fish and cook for 1½ minutes. After adding remaining ingredients reheat for 30–45 seconds.

─────── COOK'S TIP ───────
Use Indian Basmati rice rather than ordinary long grain. Its distinctive aroma and taste accentuates the recipe's Indian origin.

Stargazy crumble (page 71) with Cherry tomato salad (page 122).

OVERLEAF
From the left clockwise: Smoked fish kebabs (page 111); Matelote Normandy (page 89); Warm seafood salad (page 50); Cream cheese and prawn croûstades (page 55).

SOUSED HERRINGS

F rom top to bottom: Carrot, coriander and coley loaf (page 73); Creamy fish korma (page 77) and Rich shellfish mousse (page 108).

Microwaving soused herring is not the lengthy procedure it normally is, neither does it mean baking hoards of the fish to avoid wasting fuel. Soft herring roes (as opposed to hard) should not be discarded during cleaning as they add flavour to the finished dish, so cook these separately in a little butter and combine before chilling. Selecting soft roed herring is not purely a matter of luck – the fishmonger can determine the type of roe by giving the belly of the fish a gentle squeeze.

Serves 2

2 small herrings, about 450 g (1 lb)
salt and freshly ground black pepper
75 ml (3 fl oz) cider or white wine vinegar
1 chilli (optional)
½ small onion, sliced
2 bay leaves
5 ml (1 level tsp) pickling spice

To serve

wholemeal bread and butter

1. Clean and gut the herrings and discard head, fins and backbone. Cut each fish into 2 fillets and season well. Roll up the fillets and secure with cocktail sticks.

2. Arrange in a small shallow dish and add remaining ingredients and 75 ml (3 fl oz) water.

3. Cover and microwave on MEDIUM for 4 minutes then leave fish to cool in the liquid. Remove cocktail sticks and chill before serving with wholemeal bread and butter.

JUGGED KIPPERS

Traditionally jugged kippers are prepared by pouring boiling water over the fillets in a jug and leaving for about 10 minutes, by which time the kippers are sufficiently cooked. In the microwave method the principle is the same, although they are cooked briefly to reduce waiting time.

Serves 2

350 g (12 oz) kipper fillets

1. Place kippers in a shallow dish and pour over 600 ml (1 pint) boiling water.

2. Cover and microwave on HIGH for 1 minute. Leave to stand in water for 2 minutes. Drain thoroughly before serving.

————— SERVING SUGGESTION —————
Serve with Granary bread or wholemeal toast and any one of the savoury butters on page 24.

MUSSELS WITH TARRAGON BUTTER

Heaped hot steaming mussels, unadulterated except for a hint of tarragon, makes irresistible snack food that takes only minutes to prepare.

Serves 2

5 ml (1 level tsp) fresh chopped tarragon or 2.5 ml (½ level tsp) dried

25 g (1 oz) butter

black pepper

5 ml (1 tsp) wine vinegar

1.2 litres (2 pints) mussels, scrubbed

To serve

crusty bread

1. Place the tarragon and butter in a large bowl. Microwave on HIGH for 1 minute until butter has melted.

2. Add the pepper, vinegar and mussels and toss well.

3. Cover and microwave on HIGH for 4 minutes until mussels have opened. Divide between large serving bowls and return any mussels which have not opened to microwave on HIGH for a further 1 minute. Discard any which remain closed.

4. Pour the mussel juices over mussels and serve with plenty of crusty bread.

To serve one
Halve the quantities of ingredients and cook as above, melting the butter for 30 seconds, and cooking the mussels for 2½–3 minutes until opened. Return any that do not open for a further 45 seconds. Discard any that still remain closed.

SMOKED SALMON WITH SCRAMBLED EGGS

The marvel of microwaved scrambled eggs is usually one of the first experiments tried out by microwave owners. A fascinating sight it may be but care is still needed to avoid overcooking the eggs to a rubbery texture. Here they are finished with cream, celery seeds and smoked salmon for the ultimate breakfast dish, or light snack.

Serves 2

knob of butter

1.5 ml ($\frac{1}{4}$ level tsp) celery seeds

4 eggs

60 ml (4 tbsp) single cream

50 g (2 oz) smoked salmon, chopped

salt and freshly ground black pepper

To serve

buttered wholemeal toast

1. Place the butter in a large bowl and microwave on HIGH for 30 seconds until melted.

2. Add the celery seeds, eggs and cream and beat well.

3. Microwave on HIGH for 1 minute, stirring twice. Add salmon and seasoning and microwave on HIGH for a further 1–2 minutes, stirring twice until eggs are still very moist but no longer runny.

4. Serve immediately with buttered toast.

TOASTED ROES

A simple snack which is a little more time consuming, but rather more nourishing than cheese on toast.

Serves 2

15 g ($\frac{1}{2}$ oz) butter or margarine

50 g (2 oz) button mushrooms

2 small pickled cucumber, diced

125 g (4 oz) can soft herring roes

15 ml (1 level tbsp) mayonnaise

salt and freshly ground black pepper

2 slices bread, toasted

25 g (1 oz) Cheddar cheese, grated

1. Place the butter or margarine in a shallow dish and microwave on HIGH for 1 minute until melted. Stir in the mushrooms and cucumber and microwave on HIGH for 1 minute.

2. Drain and cut the roes into large pieces.

3. Beat the mayonnaise and seasoning into the mushroom mixture. Carefully fold in the roes.

4. Pile mixture onto the bread and sprinkle with the grated cheese. Microwave on HIGH for 1 minute until heated through.

OYSTER CANAPES

Although designed as an easy summertime snack (with a lightly dressed mixed salad) these finger morsels might equally well be served with pre-dinner drinks – a welcome change to the more traditional-style canapes.

Makes 18

3 large thin slices bread, toasted
105 g (3.66 oz) can smoked oysters
50 g (2 oz) blue brie

Garnish

mustard and cress

1. Cut each slice of bread into 6 rectangles, discarding crusts.

2. Drain oysters on kitchen paper and place one on each piece of bread. Arrange canapes in two circles on a flat serving plate, keeping centre of plate empty.

3. Cut cheese into small pieces and place over oysters. Microwave, uncovered, on HIGH for 30–45 seconds until cheese has slightly melted.

4. Garnish centre of plate with mustard and cress.

MAIN
COURSES

MUSTARD MACKEREL

A piquant mustard sauce goes beautifully with the smooth, rich taste of mackerel. If you can get them 'Horse Mackerel' or 'Scad' make a good substitute, for smaller portions.

Serves 4

4 small mackerel, cleaned and gutted

600 ml (1 pint) Court Bouillon (see page 30)

15 ml (1 level tbsp) tomato purée

10 ml (2 level tsp) coarse grain mustard

salt and freshly ground black pepper

1. Score the mackerel down each side with a sharp knife and lay in a large shallow dish.

2. Pour the Court Bouillon over the fish. Cover and microwave on HIGH for 6–7 minutes until mackerel is cooked through, turning fish over half way through cooking.

3. Transfer mackerel to warmed serving plates and cover with foil.

4. Strain the cooking juices into a bowl and stir in the tomato purée, mustard and seasoning. Microwave on HIGH for about 1 minute until heated through. Serve spooned over the fish.

—— COOK'S TIP ——
Any leftovers should not be discarded. Rich and meaty mackerel is delicious cold in sandwiches with mayonnaise and tomatoes.

FISH TIMBALE

Steamed suet puddings that cook on the hob for hours (and monopolise your time well before dinner) need less than 10 minutes. The suet case encloses a delicious cod and mushroom filling, flavoured with pickled walnuts to add a little 'bite'. These are usually available in jars from large supermarkets.

Serves 4–5

Filling

3 pickled walnuts

½ onion, peeled and chopped

100 g (4 oz) button mushrooms, sliced

100 g (4 oz) long grain rice

300 ml (½ pint) fish stock, fish fumet or water

salt and freshly ground black pepper

450 g (1 lb) cod fillet

Pastry

225 g (8 oz) self-raising flour

1.5 ml (¼ level tsp) ground turmeric

100 g (4 oz) shredded suet

1. Roughly chop the pickled walnuts. Mix together the onion, mushrooms, walnuts, rice, stock or water and seasoning in a shallow dish.

2. Cover and microwave on HIGH for 10 minutes stirring once until the liquid has been absorbed.

3. Cut the cod into chunks, discarding skin and bones and stir into the rice mixture.

4. Make the pastry: sift the flour, turmeric and a pinch of salt into a bowl. Add the suet and about 150 ml (¼ pint) water to mix to a firm dough.

5. Reserve a quarter for lid and roll out the remainder to line the base and sides of a greased 1.45 litres (2½ pints) pudding basin. Spoon the filling into centre.

6. Dampen pastry around the top of the basin with water. Roll out reserved pastry to a circle and position for lid. Cover and microwave on HIGH for 8 minutes.

7. Leave to stand for 5 minutes then invert onto a serving plate.

STARGAZY CRUMBLE

Microwaved pastry cannot compete with the real thing so I have used an oatmeal crumble instead. Surprisingly rich, the finished dish only requires a simple salad accompaniment.

Serves 4

8 small sardines, cleaned and gutted

1 large onion, peeled and sliced

4 rashers streaky bacon, chopped

15 ml (1 tbsp) oil

5 ml (1 level tsp) coarse grain mustard

30 ml (2 level tbsp) fresh chopped parsley

salt and freshly ground black pepper

Crumble

50 g (2 oz) plain flour

50 g (2 oz) coarse oatmeal

50 g (2 oz) butter or margarine

Garnish

leaf parsley or basil

1. Cut fins and tail off fish. Snip through backbone, behind the head, then pull out backbone completely.

2. Place the onion and bacon in a dish with the oil. Cover and microwave on HIGH for 5 minutes, stirring once. Stir in the mustard, parsley and seasoning.

3. Arrange the sardines in a spiral, on a 25 cm (10 in) plate with the heads to outside of dish. Spread the sardines with the onion mixture.

4. Make the crumble: place the flour, oatmeal and a pinch of salt in a bowl. Add the fat, cut into small pieces and rub in with the fingertips until mixture resembles breadcrumbs.

5. Sprinkle over the pie and press down lightly. Cover loosely and microwave on HIGH for 7 minutes. Uncover and microwave on HIGH for a further 3 minutes. Leave to stand for 5 minutes.

6. Serve garnished with leaf parsley or basil.

—— COOK'S TIP ——

It can be difficult to arrange large sardines in the appropriate 'spiral' fashion. If you cannot buy small specimens cut off tail ends and wedge in between the head ends.

See photograph page 61

RED MULLET EN PAPILLOTE

★ *An even simpler version of the previous recipe. Here, pinky red mullet and emerald green leek make a beautiful combination in colour and flavour.*

Serves 4

4 small red mullet, cleaned and gutted
15 g (½ oz) butter
½ leek (outer green end), finely sliced
salt and freshly ground black pepper

1. Cut out 4 rounds of greaseproof paper about 25 cm (10 in) in diameter. Smear centres with the butter.

2. Score the fish on each side using a sharp knife.

3. Arrange the sliced leeks over one half of each circle of greaseproof. Season lightly Place the fish over the leeks, seasoning inside and out.

4. Fold over the paper to enclose the fish. Roll and fold the cut edges together to seal.

5. Arrange the parcels in the microwave, overlapping the parcels (but not the fish) if necessary. Microwave on HIGH for 3½ minutes. Leave to stand for 2 minutes before serving.

── COOK'S TIP ──
The red mullet's liver is quite a delicacy and should be retained when the fish is gutted. Ask the fishmonger to bear this in mind.

SALMON EN PAPILLOTE WITH LIGHT GINGER BUTTER

★ *Cooking 'en papillote' is a well-established, exciting, and rewarding style of cooking in which ingredients are both cooked and served in tightly wrapped paper parcels so that each diner enjoys their first aroma of the enclosed delicacy as the bag is pierced open.*

Serves 6

7.5 cm (3 in) piece fresh root ginger
40 g (1½ oz) butter
6 salmon steaks
15 ml (1 tbsp) syrup from a jar of stem ginger
salt and freshly ground black pepper
pared rind of 1 orange
30 ml (2 tbsp) orange juice
12 prawns or uncooked mussels or Venus clams

Garnish

sprigs of fennel or dill

1. Peel and cut ginger into matchstick-sized pieces.

2. Cut out 6 rounds of greaseproof paper about 25 cm (10 in) in diameter. Smear centres lavishly with the butter.

3. Lay a salmon steak over one half of each circle of greaseproof so that other half can be eventually folded over to enclose filling.

4. Brush salmon with syrup and season lightly. Lay strips of ginger over salmon and cover with a piece of pared orange rind and the juice. Arrange 2 prawns, mussels or clams beside each steak, then fold over paper to enclose filling. Roll and fold the two edges together to seal the bag.

5. Arrange 3 parcels in the microwave and cook on HIGH for 3 minutes. Leave to stand while cooking the remaining 3 parcels.

6. Transfer to serving plates and garnish.

See photograph page 81

CARROT, CORIANDER AND COLEY LOAF

A simple combination of ingredients that turns coley into delicious family fare. If unattainable fresh coriander can be substituted by a generous sprinkling of ground coriander seeds.

Serves 4

350 g (12 oz) carrots, peeled and chopped
1 large potato, peeled and diced
450 g (1 lb) coley fillets
10 ml (2 level tsp) fresh chopped coriander
2.5 ml ($\frac{1}{2}$ level tsp) ground turmeric
salt and freshly ground pepper
$\frac{1}{4}$ cucumber

Garnish

coriander or leaf parsley (optional)

1. Place the carrots in a dish with 30 ml (2 tbsp) water. Cover and microwave on HIGH for 5 minutes until almost tender. Add the potato and cook for a further 4 minutes until completely tender.

2. Cut the coley into chunks, discarding skin and bones. Cover and microwave on HIGH for 3 minutes.

3. Stir the coriander, turmeric and seasoning into the carrot mixture and mash well. Stir in the fish.

4. Place the mixture in a 1.2 litre (2 pint) dish and level surface. Decorate attractively with overlapping slices of cucumber. Cover and microwave on HIGH for 2 minutes or until heated through. Garnish with coriander or parsley.

See photograph page 64

'ROAST' MONKFISH WITH GARLIC

★ A large tail piece of monkfish, weighing up to about 1.35 kg (3 lb) can be conventionally roasted for which it has attained the name 'Gijot de Mer'. Pasted with garlic and rosemary and seared in a browning dish the microwave variation is just as delicious, if a little extravagant.

Serves 4

700 g (1 $\frac{1}{2}$ lb) monkfish tail
2 garlic cloves, skinned and crushed
2.5 ml ($\frac{1}{2}$ level tsp) fresh chopped rosemary or 1.5 ml ($\frac{1}{4}$ level tsp) dried
salt and freshly ground black pepper
2.5 ml ($\frac{1}{2}$ level tsp) plain flour
15 ml (1 tbsp) olive oil

1. Cut any thick membrane from around the monkfish and discard the central bone to leave two separate pieces of meat. Tie pieces together with the string. Dry the fish thoroughly on kitchen paper.

2. Mix together the garlic, rosemary and seasoning and spread over the surface of the fish. Dust lightly with the flour.

3. Preheat a browning dish following the manufacturer's directions. Add oil. Place fish in the browning dish and turn in oil until sizzling dies down.

4. Cover dish and microwave on HIGH for 4 minutes until cooked through.

CHILLI FISH

In this recipe I have simply substituted fish for the more familiar meat in a chilli-based sauce. The result is lighter and more interesting particularly if served in crisp 'Taco' shells.

Serves 4

450 g (1 lb) coley fillet
5 ml (1 tsp) oil
1 onion, peeled and chopped
1 garlic glove, skinned and crushed
5 ml (1 level tsp) mild chilli powder
227 g (8 oz) can chopped tomatoes
397 g (14 oz) can red kidney beans
30 ml (2 level tbsp) tomato purée
2.5 ml ($\frac{1}{2}$ level tsp) fresh chopped oregano or 1.5 ml ($\frac{1}{4}$ level tsp) dried
salt and freshly ground pepper
8 Taco shells

Garnish

avocado slices
soured cream
ground paprika

1. Cut the fish into small chunks, discarding skin and bones.

2. Place the oil, onion, garlic and chilli powder in a dish and microwave on HIGH for 2 minutes.

3. Stir in the fish, tomatoes, drained beans, tomato purée, oregano and seasoning. Cover and microwave on HIGH for 5 minutes, stirring once.

4. Spoon the mixture into Taco shells and arrange on a plate. Cover with kitchen paper and microwave on HIGH for 1–2 minutes until heated through.

5. Garnish with avocado slices and spoonfuls of soured cream, and sprinkle with paprika.

See photograph page 104

SCAMPI, MUSHROOM AND AVOCADO BROCHETTES

★ *I have to admit to disappointment the first time I tried this recipe. I used a pack of frozen scampi and was horrified at the amount of 'meat' left once the protective 'ice glaze' had melted. Do not make the same error – if only frozen is available use whole prawns instead, and peel them before skewering.*

Serves 4

1 ripe avocado
350 g (12 oz) scampi, peeled
100 g (4 oz) small button mushrooms
2.5 ml ($\frac{1}{2}$ level tsp) fresh chopped oregano, or 1.5 ml ($\frac{1}{4}$ level tsp) dried
15 ml (1 tbsp) lemon or lime juice
15 g ($\frac{1}{2}$ oz) butter, melted
salt and freshly ground black pepper
15 ml (1 tbsp) brandy
60 ml (4 tbsp) double cream
15 ml (1 level tbsp) fresh chopped parsley

1. Peel and dice the avocado. Alternate with the scampi and mushrooms on 4 wooden skewers. Arrange in a shallow dish.

2. Mix together the oregano, lemon or lime juice, butter and a little seasoning. Brush over the kebabs.

3. Cover loosely and microwave on HIGH for 1$\frac{1}{2}$–2 minutes until the mushrooms are slightly softened. Drain the kebabs to a serving dish and keep warm.

4. Add the brandy, cream and parsley to the juices and microwave on HIGH for 45 seconds to 1 minute until heated through. Turn out into a sauceboat and serve separately.

SWEDISH HERRINGS

The Swedes use a sweet, pungent mustard that goes beautifully with fish. Difficult to obtain here it can be imitated by sweetening English mustard for use as the basis of marinade. Hot steaming potatoes make an authentic accompaniment.

Serves 4

$\frac{1}{2}$ cucumber
4 small herrings, gutted
5 ml (1 level tsp) English mustard
10 ml (2 level tsp) caster sugar
45 ml (3 tbsp) white wine vinegar
5 ml (1 level tsp) fresh chopped dill or 2.5 ml ($\frac{1}{2}$ level tsp) dried
salt and freshly ground black pepper
soured cream

1. Slice the cucumber and arrange in a large shallow dish.

2. Score the herrings down sides and lay over the cucumber.

3. Mix together the mustard, sugar, vinegar, dill and seasoning and spoon over the fish. Cover and leave to marinate for 30 minutes.

4. Microwave on HIGH for 4–5 minutes, turning fish over and re-arranging half way through cooking time.

5. Leave to stand for 3 minutes and serve with spoonfuls of soured cream.

MONKFISH WITH GIN AND LIME

★ *A refreshing combination of flavours that I can recommend on a warm summer's evening. Prettily garnished with lime and pistachio nuts, a colourful platter of fresh summer vegetables is all that is needed to complete the meal.*

Serves 4

3 limes
700 g (1½ lb) monkfish
15 ml (1 tbsp) oil
2 shallots, peeled and finely chopped
60 ml (4 tbsp) Gin
salt and ground white pepper
15 g (½ oz) butter, softened
15 ml (1 level tbsp) plain flour

Garnish

pistachio nuts

1. Pare thin strips of rind from the limes. Cut strips into fine shreds. Place in a bowl of boiling water. Squeeze the juice from the limes and reserve.

2. Cut the monkfish into cubes.

3. Preheat a browning dish following manufacturer's directions. Add the oil, shallots and fish and turn in the dish until sizzling dies down. Cover and microwave on HIGH for 1 minute, stirring once.

4. Add Gin, lime juice and seasoning and microwave on HIGH for 1 minute.

5. Blend the butter and flour to a smooth paste. Whisk into the juices in dish. Cover and microwave on HIGH for a further 1–2 minutes, whisking several times until juices have thickened.

6. Cover and leave to stand for 3 minutes. Serve garnished with shredded lime and pistachio nuts.

FISH ROULADES WITH HAZELNUTS AND CAPERS

By the time small flat fish fillets are cooked there is usually little more than a mouthful to eat – unless they are first stuffed.
Rolling the fillets does take a little time so prepare them in advance and arrange in a suitable dish, ready for last minute cooking.

Serves 4

50 g (2 oz) hazelnuts
30 ml (2 level tbsp) capers
15 g (½ oz) butter or margarine
25 g (1 oz) breadcrumbs
good pinch ground nutmeg
salt and freshly ground black pepper
8 large plaice fillets (about 700 g [1½ lb] in total weight)
150 ml (¼ pint) dry white wine, fish stock or fumet
1 bay leaf

1. Chop the hazelnuts and capers fairly finely.

2. Place the butter or margarine in a bowl and microwave on HIGH for 1 minute, until melted. Stir in the hazelnuts, capers, breadcrumbs, nutmeg and a little seasoning.

3. Wipe the fish fillets and place, skinned sides down, on a board. Spoon the stuffing over fillets. Roll up the fillets and secure each with a cocktail stick. Transfer to a shallow dish.

4. Pour the white wine or stock over the fish. Break the bay leaf and add to dish.

5. Cover and microwave on HIGH for 6 minutes or until fish flakes easily when pierced with a knife. Cover and leave to stand for 3 minutes before serving.

------ SERVING SUGGESTION ------
Pilau or ordinary rice makes the ideal accompaniment as the cooking juices can be spooned over when serving.
If you have any cream in the fridge, stir 30–40 ml (2–3 tbsp) into the cooking juices and reheat gently in the microwave for a slightly richer sauce.

CREAMY FISH KORMA

I can never see the point in smothering delicately flavoured seafood in powerful spice. Here, everyday fish is coated in a gingery almond sauce to accentuate rather than kill the natural flavour.

Serves 4

2.5 cm (1 in) piece fresh root ginger
450 g (1 lb) cod, haddock or coley fillets
150 ml ($\frac{1}{4}$ pint) natural yogurt
2 garlic cloves, skinned and crushed
2.5 ml ($\frac{1}{2}$ level tsp) ground turmeric
15 ml (1 tbsp) oil
1 onion, peeled and chopped
2.5 ml ($\frac{1}{2}$ level tsp) ground coriander
7.5 cm (3 in) piece cinnamon stick
1.5 ml ($\frac{1}{4}$ level tbsp) mild chilli powder
15 ml (1 level tbsp) tomato purée
50 g (2 oz) ground almonds
100 g (4 oz) peeled prawns
150 ml ($\frac{1}{4}$ pint) single cream
salt and freshly ground black pepper

Garnish

toasted almonds

1. Peel and chop the ginger. Cut the fish into large chunks, discarding skin and bones.

2. Mix together the yogurt, garlic, turmeric and ginger and spoon over the fish. Cover and leave to marinate for 1 hour.

3. Place the oil, onion, coriander, cinnamon and chilli powder in a large shallow dish. Cover and microwave on HIGH for 3 minutes, stirring once.

4. Add the fish, marinade, tomato purée and almonds. Cover and microwave on HIGH for 4 minutes, carefully stirring the mixture once.

5. Stir in the prawns, cream and seasoning to taste. Microwave on HIGH for a further 1–2 minutes until heated through. Leave to stand for 3 minutes.

6. Serve hot, sprinkled with toasted almonds.

See photograph page 64

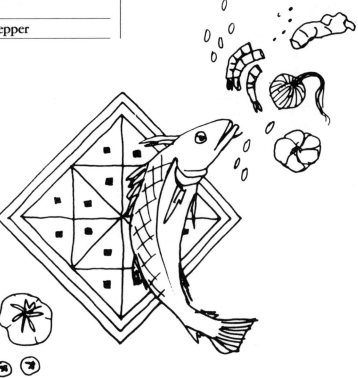

POACHED SALMON

★ *Strictly speaking, this is not a 'poached' recipe, as the fish microwaves in its own moisture without any additional cooking liquid. However the resulting appearance and moist texture is equally as good; and the flavour even better. If the fish is too large to fit into the microwave cut off the head and cook this on the plate alongside the fish. It can then be re-assembled when arranging for the table.*

Whereas a cold poached salmon makes a fabulous centrepiece for a buffet table, a hot salmon may be preferred for a small gathering. For obvious reasons, the decoration must be kept very simple, perhaps a flourish of parsley, around the salmon's head. Use the recipe below and serve as soon as the salmon is skinned.

Serves 6 for a main course
       10 for a buffet

1.35 kg (3 lb) salmon or salmon trout, cleaned and gutted
salt and freshly ground black pepper
50 g (2 oz) butter
1 packet aspic jelly powder
¼ cucumber, thinly sliced
flat leaf parsley

1. Sprinkle the fish inside and out with salt and pepper and lay on a flat plate, or on the removable turntable of the microwave. Dot the salmon liberally with butter.

2. Cover and microwave on HIGH for 5 minutes. Turn the fish over and microwave on HIGH for a further 5–6 minutes until cooked through. Leave to stand for 5 minutes.

3. Slit just through the skin along the back of the fish and around the head so that the skin can be peeled off. Turn the fish, skinned side down, onto a serving plate. Peel off the skin on the remaining side. Using a knife, gently scrape away any thin layers of brown 'curd' that cover the pink flesh.

4. Make up the aspic jelly powder following packet directions and leave until syrupy. Brush the salmon with a thin layer of aspic, then arrange the cucumber slices, overlapping at head and tail ends to represent scales. Carefully brush a second layer of aspic over the cucumber and exposed flesh, (the remaining aspic can be used to flood the plate). Garnish the head end with a large sprig of parsley.

─── SERVING SUGGESTION ───
Whether serving the salmon hot or cold keep the accompaniments simple. Suitable sauces include:– Hollandaise Sauce (page 31); Watercress Sauce (page 32); Mayonnaise (page 125); Savoury Butter (page 124) for hot poached salmon; New potatoes and a mixed salad make perfectly good accompaniments, or try one of the following:– Scallop Shell Potatoes (page 118); Fennel Salad with Bel Paese Dressing (page 122); Cherry Tomato Salad (page 122); Stir Fried Courgettes and Mushrooms (page 117); Sesame Beans with Crispy Fried Bacon (page 117).

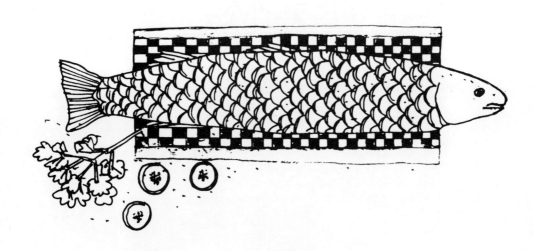

GOUGONS OF WHITING WITH MUSHROOMS

Combining smoked and unsmoked fish adds colour and interest to the simplest recipe. Surprisingly the smokey flavour does not overpower the unsmoked fish, provided it is freshly cooked and eaten without reheating.

Serves 2

---

175 g (6 oz) whiting fillet

175 g (6 oz) whiting fillet, smoked

salt and freshly ground black pepper

10 ml (2 level tsp) cornflour

15 g ($\frac{1}{2}$ oz) butter or margarine

1 bunch spring onions, trimmed and chopped

100 g (4 oz) button mushrooms, halved

150 ml ($\frac{1}{4}$ pint) milk

---

1. Remove skin and bones from whiting and cut into long thin strips. Lightly season 5 ml (1 level tsp) of the cornflour and use to coat the pieces of fish.

2. Place the butter or margarine in a shallow dish and microwave on HIGH for 1 minute until melted.

3. Toss the fish in the melted fat. Cover and microwave on HIGH for 2$\frac{1}{2}$ minutes until cooked through, carefully turning the fish once.

4. Drain the fish to a warmed serving dish. Add the spring onions and mushrooms to the dish and microwave on HIGH for 1 minute.

5. Blend the remaining 5 ml (1 level tsp) cornflour with a little of the milk.

6. Add to the mushroom mixture with the remaining milk. Cover and microwave on HIGH for 3 minutes, whisking twice until slightly thickened. Season to taste and pour over the fish.

—— COOK'S TIP ——
Absolutely fresh fish is required for cutting into 'Gougons' (as above), otherwise the pieces will fall apart during cooking.

TUNA TERIAKI

★ *'Teriaki' is a Japanese-style of cooking in which steak (normally beef) is marinated in, and then cooked with, a rich soy sauce glaze. Meaty fish steaks, particularly tuna, are delicious cooked in this way, as is swordfish or shark.*

Serves 4

---

4 small tuna steaks (about 700 g [1$\frac{1}{2}$ lb) in total weight)

45 ml (3 tbsp) soy sauce

30 ml (2 tbsp) medium sherry or mirin

1 garlic clove, skinned and crushed

1 cm ($\frac{1}{2}$ in) piece fresh root ginger, peeled and finely chopped

freshly ground black pepper

2.5 ml ($\frac{1}{2}$ level tsp) cornflour

---

1. Place the tuna steaks on a large flat plate. Mix together the soy sauce, sherry or mirin, garlic, ginger and pepper. Spoon over the fish and leave to marinate for 1–2 hours.

2. Cover and microwave on HIGH for 3 minutes. Turn the fish over and cook on HIGH for a further 4–6 minutes until cooked through.

3. Drain the fish to warmed serving plates. Cover and leave to stand while finishing the sauce.

4. Blend the cornflour with 15 ml (1 tbsp) of the cooking juices. Add to remaining juices and cook for 1 minute until slightly thickened, whisking twice.

5. Spoon the sauce over the fish before serving.

FISH BIYILDI

The tiresome process of cooking aubergines conventionally becomes a thing of the past with this easy microwave method. In mere minutes the flesh is softened, yet retains its shape and moisture ready for further preparation. White fish and spicy tomatoes make a delicious stuffing, finished with a topping of stringy melted cheese.

Serves 4

2 × 300 g (10 oz) aubergines
10 ml (2 tsp) olive oil
350 g (12 oz) cod or haddock fillet
1 onion, peeled and chopped
1 garlic clove, skinned and crushed
227 g (8 oz) can chopped tomatoes
15 ml (1 level tbsp) fresh chopped parsley
1.5 ml (¼ level tsp) ground allspice
pinch of caster sugar
salt and freshly ground black pepper
50 g (2 oz) Gruyére or Cheddar cheese, grated

1. Wipe the aubergines and cut off stalk ends. Prick over aubergines with a fork and brush with a little of the oil. Microwave on HIGH for 5–6 minutes, turning aubergines after 3 minutes, until just tender. Halve the aubergines lengthways and scoop out the centres. Roughly chop centres and reserve.

2. Cut the fish into chunks, discarding skin and bones.

3. Place the onion in a bowl with the garlic and remaining oil. Cover and microwave on HIGH for 2 minutes.

4. Stir in the tomatoes, fish, chopped aubergine centres, parsley, allspice, sugar and seasoning. Cover and microwave on HIGH for 5 minutes, stirring once.

5. Spoon the mixture into the aubergine skins and sprinkle with the grated cheese. Microwave on HIGH for 4–5 minutes until the cheese has melted and aubergines are heated through.

See photograph page 41

Salmon 'en papillote' with light ginger butter (page 72), and Stir-fried courgettes and mushrooms (page 117).

OVERLEAF
From left to right: Mediterranean salt cod (page 85); Fish cassoulet (page 110) and Pasta in pepperpool sauce (page 97).

From top to bottom: Clam salad (page 120); Seafood pizza (page 105) and Shredded skate salad with devilled dressing (page 98).

MEDITERRANEAN SALT COD

Salt cod may look rather unappetising as it hangs in hard greyish white boards at the fishmongers or delicatessen but the transformation after soaking and cooking is remarkable. I still find it too leathery to skin and bone after soaking (as most recipes suggest) and so leave this until after cooking.

Serves 4–5

---

700 g (1½ lb) salt cod

2 garlic cloves, skinned and crushed

1 onion, peeled and sliced

2 sticks of celery, sliced

45 ml (3 tbsp) olive oil

400 g (14 oz) can plum tomatoes

2.5 ml (½ level tsp) caster sugar

30 ml (2 level tbsp) tomato purée

2 bay leaves

2 small sprigs of fresh rosemary or 1.5 ml (¼ level tsp) dried

1 yellow or red pepper, sliced

salt and freshly ground black pepper

Garnish

sprigs of rosemary (optional)

1. To soak the cod, place in a large bowl, cover with water and leave for 48 hours, changing the water several times. Drain cod and cut into portion-sized pieces.

2. Place the garlic, onion, celery and oil in a large bowl. Cover and microwave on HIGH for 4 minutes, stirring once.

3. Add the tomatoes, sugar, tomato purée, bay leaves, rosemary and cod. Cover and microwave on HIGH for 15–20 minutes, rearranging the fish twice, until tender. Drain the fish and remove the skin and bones.

4. Return the flesh to the dish with the sliced pepper and seasoning. Cover and microwave on HIGH for a further 3 minutes.

5. Leave to stand for 3 minutes.

See photograph page 82

TURBOT MOUSSES WITH PRAWN TARTARE

★*Everyday teacups make perfect moulds for these creamy fish mousses, concealing a delicious prawn salad. Turbot, although expensive, tastes superb but cheaper white fish such as cod or haddock can be substituted.*

Serves 6

350 g (12 oz) whole prawns
3 small gherkins, chopped
15 ml (1 level tbsp) capers, chopped
15 ml (1 level tbsp) fresh chopped parsley
30 ml (2 level tbsp) mayonnaise
150 ml (¼ pint) single cream
salt and freshly ground black pepper
450 g (1 lb) turbot
2 egg whites

Garnish

parsley

1. Reserve 4 of the prawns for garnish and peel the remainder. Mix in a bowl with the gherkins, capers, parsley, mayonnaise, 30 ml (2 tbsp) of the cream and seasoning.

2. Roughly chop the fish, discarding skin and bones.

3. Place the fish in a liquidizer or food processor with the egg whites and blend until smooth.

4. Turn the mixture into a bowl and beat in the remaining cream and plenty of seasoning.

5. Divide the mixture among 4 lightly buttered cups using a teaspoon to make cavities in the centres. Spoon the prawn mixture into the centres and cover each cup.

6. Place in the microwave spaced slightly apart, and microwave on HIGH for 3½ minutes.

7. Leave to stand for 2 minutes, then invert onto serving plates. Serve garnished with prawns and parsley.

SERVING SUGGESTION

Watercress Sauce (page 32) or Pink Seafood Sauce (page 35) would make ideal accompaniments.

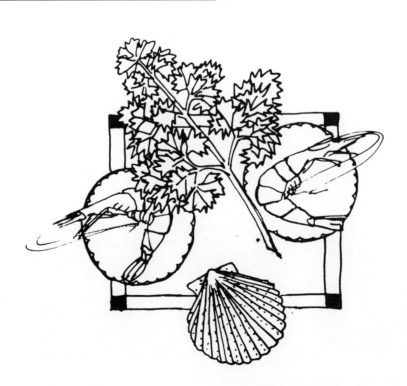

BACON WRAPPED MULLET

Because of its sheer good value, mullet can be enjoyed as an everyday meal, making a change to the less obvious choices of cod, haddock, mackerel etc. If gutting the fish at home, keep the roe and put it in the stuffing for added flavour and goodness.

Serves 3–4

25 g (1 oz) butter or margarine
1 small onion, peeled and chopped
50 g (2 oz) breadcrumbs
5 ml (1 level tsp) fresh chopped sage or 2.5 ml ($\frac{1}{2}$ level tsp) dried
$\frac{1}{2}$ small red pepper, finely chopped
salt and freshly ground black pepper
900 g (2 lb) grey mullet, cleaned and gutted
4 long rashers of streaky bacon

To serve

600 ml (1 pint) Rich Tomato Sauce (see page 32)

1. Place the butter in a bowl and microwave on HIGH for 1 minute until melted. Stir in the onion, cover and microwave on HIGH for 2 minutes until softened.

2. Stir in the breadcrumbs, sage, red pepper and seasoning.

3. Score the fish down both sides using a sharp knife. Spoon the stuffing into the cavity.

4. Stretch the bacon rashers with the back of a knife and wrap around the fish, securing ends with cocktail sticks.

5. Place the fish on a flat plate and cover with kitchen paper. Microwave on HIGH for 5 minutes. Turn fish over, re-cover with kitchen paper and microwave on HIGH for a further 4–5 minutes until cooked through.

6. Leave to stand, covered, for 3–4 minutes. Serve with Rich Tomato Sauce.

See photograph page 102

SEA BASS IN A SALT CRUST

★ A traditionally baked recipe that adapts well to the microwave. The fish is cooked under a thick blanket of salt which is removed after cooking along with the skin to reveal a highly seasoned and moist white flesh. Serve with new potatoes and a mixed vegetable dish such as Ratatouille (page 116) to add colour.

Serves 5–6

1.36 kg (3 lb) sea bass, cleaned and gutted
3 garlic cloves, skinned
$\frac{1}{2}$ lemon, sliced
few sprigs of parsley
few sprigs of rosemary or thyme
225 g (8 oz) sea salt

1. Open out the cavity of the bass and fill with the garlic cloves, lemon slices, parsley and rosemary or thyme.

2. Sprinkle a third of the salt into a shallow dish or plate. Place the fish on top and cover with kitchen paper.

3. Microwave on HIGH for 5 minutes. Turn fish over and sprinkle with the remaining salt. Cover with kitchen paper and microwave on HIGH for a further 5 minutes.

4. Cover with foil and leave to stand for 5 minutes before serving.

––––– COOK'S TIP –––––

This is the one recipe in which a whole round fish is not scored down each side before cooking. This would allow the salt to penetrate the flesh giving an unpleasantly salty flavour.

BRAISED COD

Semi-submerged in a scarlet red sauce, buttered cod steaks look highly appetising. Filleted white fish makes a cheaper substitute for family meals – a good way of livening up those ever useful frozen 'slabs'.

Serves 4

2 rashers streaky bacon, chopped
1 bunch spring onions, trimmed and chopped
397 g (14 oz) can chopped tomatoes
30 ml (2 level tbsp) tomato ketchup
8 gherkins, halved
2 bay leaves
2.5 ml (½ level tsp) fresh chopped thyme or 1.5 ml (¼ level tsp) dried
salt and freshly ground black pepper
4 small cod steaks (about 570 g [1¼ lb] in total weight)
knob of butter or margarine

1. Place the bacon and spring onions in a large shallow dish. Cover and microwave on HIGH for 3 minutes, stirring once.

2. Stir in the tomatoes, ketchup, gherkins, bay leaves, thyme and seasoning.

3. Lay the cod over the tomato mixture. Season lightly and dot with butter. Cover and microwave on HIGH for 5 minutes or until cod is cooked through, re-arranging steaks once.

4. Leave to stand for 5 minutes.

FISH PIE

With celeriac added to the potato and a soft blue brie topping, this recipe is more exciting than the traditional fish pie. However, you can always play safe and substitute a Cheddar cheese sauce, and extra potato for the celeriac.

Serves 4

350 g (12 oz) celeriac, peeled and roughly chopped
450 g (1 lb) potatoes, peeled and roughly chopped
15 g (½ oz) butter or margarine
salt and freshly ground black pepper
450 g (1 lb) cod, haddock or coley fillets
300 ml (½ pint) Blue Brie Sauce (see page 31)
100 g (4 oz) frozen peas
15 ml (1 level tbsp) Parmesan cheese

1. Place celeriac and potatoes in a dish with 30 ml (2 tbsp) water. Cover and microwave on HIGH for 8 minutes until tender, turning twice. Mash with the butter or margarine and seasoning until smooth.

2. Place fish in a shallow dish and season lightly. Cover and microwave on HIGH for 5 minutes, turning once until just cooked. Drain fish, adding juices to Blue Brie Sauce.

3. Roughly flake fish, discarding skin and bones.

4. Arrange half the fish and peas in a shallow pie dish. Cover with half the potato mixture. Top with remaining fish and peas, then remaining potato mixture. Cover with sauce and sprinkle with Parmesan.

5. Cover and microwave on HIGH for 5 minutes. Uncover and microwave on HIGH for a further 3 minutes. Leave to stand for 3 minutes before serving.

MATELOTE NORMANDY

There are umpteen variations of this tasty fish stew associated with northern France. The fish used can be a mixture, or one on its own, depending on what takes your fancy when buying. I have used brill, a classic ingredient of a 'Matelote', but as it is difficult to buy you may prefer to substitute another firm-textured white fish.

Serves 4–6

700 g (1½ lb) brill
25 g (1 oz) butter
1 onion, peeled and chopped
25 g (1 oz) plain flour
300 ml (½ pint) dry cider
10 ml (2 level tsp) coarse grain mustard
2 dessert apples, cored and sliced
30 ml (2 level tbsp) fresh chopped parsley
salt and freshly ground black pepper
600 ml (1 pint) mussels, scrubbed

Garnish

extra parsley

1. Cut the fish into chunks, discarding skin and bones.

2. Place butter in a large bowl. Cover and microwave on HIGH for 1 minute until melted. Add onion and microwave on HIGH for 2 minutes.

3. Stir in flour and cook on HIGH for 1 minute. Gradually blend in cider and mustard. Cover and microwave on HIGH for 2 minutes, stirring once until slightly thickened.

4. Add brill and apples and cook on HIGH for 4 minutes, stirring once until just cooked. Add parsley, seasoning and mussels and microwave on HIGH for a further 3 minutes until mussels have opened. Microwave any mussels which have not opened for a further 1 minute. Discard any mussels which still remain closed.

5. Serve sprinkled with extra parsley.

See photograph page 63

OCTOPUS STEW

★ *However tender the octopus you buy (see page 15) it needs a preliminary cooking which is best done on the hob. First cut through the octopus above and below the eyes and discard this part. Turn the head inside out and discard contents. Slice head and tentacles and place in a little salted water over the lowest possible heat. After 30 minutes to 1 hour of gently simmering, the flesh will be deliciously tender and ready to use in a stew such as this.*

Serves 4

15 ml (1 tbsp) oil
1 onion, peeled and chopped
1 garlic clove, skinned and crushed
15 ml (1 level tbsp) plain flour
700 g (1½ lb) octopus, prepared and tenderised
397 g (14 oz) can plum tomatoes
30 ml (2 level tbsp) tomato purée
2.5 ml (½ level tsp) caster sugar
12 black olives
salt and freshly ground black pepper

Garnish

fresh chopped parsley

1. Preheat a browning dish following manufacturer's directions. Add the oil, onion and garlic and stir until sizzling dies down.

2. Stir in the flour, then octopus pieces (already tenderised), tomatoes, tomato purée, sugar, olives and seasoning. Cover and microwave on HIGH for 10 minutes, stirring twice.

3. Leave to stand for 3 minutes then serve sprinkled with parsley.

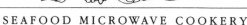

SEA BREAM WITH CHERMOULA

★ *'Chermoula' is an aromatic and colourful, spicy paste that is pressed onto both sides of a whole fish and left to marinate so that the flesh can absorb the wonderful taste. I used a smallish sea bream to serve four but you could try mullet, hake, redfish or sea bass. A 1.35 kg (3 lb) specimen would serve six and make a marvellous buffet centrepiece. Simply extend the cooking time by about 3 minutes.*

Serves 4

900 g (2 lb) sea bream, cleaned and gutted

1.5 ml ($\frac{1}{4}$ level tsp) crushed saffron strands, soaked for several hours in 15 ml (1 tbsp) boiling water, or a good pinch of ground turmeric

$\frac{1}{2}$ onion, peeled and finely chopped

2 garlic cloves, skinned and crushed

30 ml (2 tbsp) olive oil

15 ml (1 level tbsp) fresh chopped coriander

30 ml (2 level tbsp) fresh chopped parsley

1.5 ml ($\frac{1}{4}$ level tsp) ground cumin

salt and freshly ground black pepper

1. Score the fish down both sides and place on a plate.

2. Beat together the saffron or turmeric, onion, garlic, oil, coriander, parsley and cumin. Season generously.

3. Press the marinade onto both sides of the fish, packing it well into the slits and body cavity. Cover loosely with cling film and leave to marinate for 2–3 hours.

4. Transfer the fish to the microwave and cook on HIGH for 2 minutes. Turn fish over and microwave on HIGH for a further 7 minutes until cooked through. Leave to stand for 5 minutes before serving.

STUFFED HAKE

★ *Hake is becoming such a rarity in the fishmongers that it should be bought at any opportunity. Stuffed with a tempting combination of pine kernals, fresh spinach and Parmesan this dish will suit the grandest or most humble occasion.*

Serves 4

4 small hake cutlets

15 g ($\frac{1}{2}$ oz) butter

1 small onion, peeled and finely chopped

1 garlic clove, skinned and crushed

75 g (3 oz) fresh spinach, washed and finely shredded

25 g (1 oz) pine kernals

30 ml (2 level tbsp) Parmesan cheese

25 g (1 oz) fresh breadcrumbs

salt and freshly ground black pepper

60 ml (4 tbsp) single cream

1. Arrange the cutlets in a large shallow dish with the cavities facing inwards.

2. Place the butter in a bowl and microwave on HIGH for 1 minute until melted. Stir in the onion and garlic. Cover and microwave on HIGH for 2 minutes until softened. Stir in the spinach, pine kernals, Parmesan cheese, breadcrumbs and seasoning.

3. Spoon the stuffing into the cavities and pour over 30 ml (2 tbsp) water. Season lightly. Cover and microwave on HIGH for 6–8 minutes until fish is cooked through.

4. Transfer fish to serving plates and cover while finishing sauce.

5. Stir the cream into the juices left in the dish. Microwave on MEDIUM for 20 seconds until heated through. Season to taste and spoon around the fish.

—— COOK'S TIP ——
The recipe works equally well with cutlets of cod or haddock. Chopped cashews or peanuts can be substituted for the pine kernals if necessary.

ORIENTAL FISH WITH STAR ANISE

★ *Whole white fish, steamed after a long marinading is a delicious Far Eastern speciality. The microwave produces a similarly moist result in about a third of the cooking time and without the precariously balanced steamer and heated kitchen.*

Serves 5–6

1.35 kg (3 lb) sea bass, sea bream or red fish, cleaned and gutted

2 garlic gloves, skinned and crushed

45 ml (3 level tbsp) tomato purée

7.5 ml (1½ level tsp) five-spice powder

20 ml (4 tsp) clear honey

20 ml (4 tsp) soy sauce

45 ml (3 tbsp) medium sherry or mirin

salt and freshly ground black pepper

Garnish

spring onion curls

star anise

star cut pieces of carrot

1. Using a sharp knife make several cuts down both sides of the fish.

2. Mix together the garlic, tomato purée, five-spice powder, honey, soy sauce, sherry or mirin and seasoning. Brush about half over both sides of the fish and leave to marinate for 1–2 hours.

3. Cover loosely and microwave on HIGH for 5 minutes. Turn fish over and microwave on HIGH for a further 5 minutes. Carefully transfer to a warmed serving dish. Cover with foil and leave to stand for 3 minutes.

4. Meanwhile stir any juices left on the cooking plate into the remaining soy sauce mixture with 30 ml (2 tbsp) water. Microwave on HIGH for 20–30 seconds until heated through. Spoon around the fish.

5. Serve garnished with spring onion curls, whole star anise and carrots.

—— COOK'S TIP ——
To make the spring onion curls, cut 2–3 trimmed spring onions into 5 cm (2 in) pieces. Cut each piece lengthways into quarters so that spring onions fall into thick shreds. Place in a bowl of iced water for at least 2 hours until prettily curled. Drain well before using.

See cover photograph

HALIBUT WITH LIGHT ALE

★*Just as brown ale gives a yeasty flavour to carbonnade, so does light ale to fish. The firm texture and distinctive flavour of halibut withstands the richness of this sauce, providing a good use for the frozen steaks (which have a tendency to 'dryness' after thawing) the only form in which halibut is available to many of us.*

Serves 4–5

350 g (12 oz) celeriac
550–700 g (1¼–1½ lb) halibut
25 g (1 oz) butter
1 large leek, sliced
30 ml (2 level tbsp) plain flour
300 ml (½ pint) light ale
150 ml (¼ pint) fish stock
2.5 ml (½ level tsp) caster sugar
salt and freshly ground black pepper

Garnish

leaf parsley

1. Peel and cut the celeriac into small cubes. Cut the halibut into large pieces discarding skin and bones.

2. Melt the butter in a large shallow dish. Add the celeriac and leek. Cover and microwave on HIGH for 5 minutes, stirring once.

3. Add the flour and microwave on HIGH for 30 seconds. Gradually blend in the ale, stock and sugar. Cover and microwave on HIGH for 2 minutes.

4. Arrange the halibut in the sauce. Cover and microwave on HIGH for 4–5 minutes, stirring once, until fish is cooked through. Season to taste and leave to stand for 3 minutes.

5. Serve garnished with parsley.

DOVER SOLE AND LETTUCE CUPS

★*In this recipe, one costly sole is cleverly stretched to serve four by cooking it in ramekins with a delicate combination of lettuce, prawns, cream and mace. I rarely recommend the flimsy round variety of lettuce but here they are essential, creating a beautiful pastel green casing around the delicious filling.*

Serves 4

1 round lettuce
60 ml (4 tbsp) single cream
½ egg, beaten
100 g (4 oz) peeled prawns
1.5 ml (¼ level tsp) ground mace
salt and freshly ground black pepper
knob of butter
1 large Dover sole, filleted and skinned

1. Reserve 8 large outer leaves from the lettuce. Weigh another 25 g (1 oz) and finely chop. Mix with the cream, beaten egg, prawns, mace and seasoning.

2. Plunge the outer leaves into boiling water for about 30 seconds, until slightly softened. Drain thoroughly. Grease 4 microwave ramekin dishes with the butter. Use lettuce leaves to line dishes so that the edges come well above the top.

3. Season the sole on both sides and pack into the ramekins, first lining the sides of each dish and letting the remaining sole line the bases.

4. Spoon the lettuce and prawn mixture into the ramekins.

5. Bring edges of the lettuce leaves over the filling. Cover the ramekins and arrange in microwave, spaced well apart. Microwave on MEDIUM for 4 minutes until filling is lightly set.

6. Leave to stand for 3 minutes then invert onto warmed serving plates.

'HOT CROSS' POTATOES

A budget-beating nutritious family tea that stretches a small amount of fish. Both the potatoes and filling can be prepared ahead and reheated just before serving.

Serves 4

4 large baking potatoes
5 ml (1 tsp) oil
salt and freshly ground black pepper
225 g (8 oz) cod or haddock fillet
15 g (½ oz) butter or margarine
1 small onion, peeled and chopped
100 g (4 oz) prawns, peeled
200 g (7 oz) Quark with onions and herbs

Garnish

fresh chopped chives
whole prawns (optional)

1. Scrub the potatoes and pierce with a fork. Brush with the oil and sprinkle with salt. Microwave on HIGH for 15–20 minutes until tender, re-arranging twice.

2. While still hot, cut deep crosses into tops of potatoes and open out slightly to provide containers for the filling.

3. Cut fish into chunks, discarding skin and bones.

4. Place butter or margarine in a shallow dish and microwave on HIGH for 1 minute until melted. Add the onion and cod or haddock and microwave on HIGH for 3 minutes.

5. Stir in the prawns, Quark and seasoning and spoon into the potato cases. Microwave on HIGH for 2–3 minutes or until heated through.

6. Garnish with chives and prawns if using.

COD STEAKS AU POIVRE

★ *Using the same principles as 'steak au Poivre' I have chosen to use pink peppercorns which are the mildest, most aromatic form of pepper and therefore compliment rather than overwhelm the fish. Exactly the same method could be used for the meatier textured swordfish or shark steaks, although the cooking time should be increased.*

Serves 4

30 ml (2 level tbsp) pink peppercorns
4 small cod steaks (about 570 g [1¼ lb] in total weight)
salt
25 g (1 oz) butter
150 ml (¼ pint) single cream

1. Crush the peppercorns as finely as possible. Thoroughly dry the cod steaks and coat on both cut sides with the peppercorns. Season lightly with salt.

2. Place the butter in a shallow dish and microwave on HIGH for 1 minute until melted. Add cod steaks.

3. Cover and microwave on HIGH for 2 minutes. Turn the fish over and cook on HIGH for a further 3–4 minutes until cooked through. Transfer steaks to warmed serving plates.

4. Add the cream to juices in pan and microwave on MEDIUM for 1 minute until heated through. Season with extra salt if necessary and pour around the fish.

See photograph page 103

DELICATE CHEESE FONDUE

★ *When you want something a little different for your next informal gathering, look no further than this extravagant fondue. Three cheeses make up the fondue itself which is served with an array of shellfish for dipping. The choice of fish is yours – a few cooked King or Dublin Bay prawns and crab claws will give an 'exotic' feel but these can be supplemented with cheaper fish such as cooked mussels or clams, small prawns or sautéed rings of squid. An additional basket of cubed crusty bread will provide an extra 'lighter' choice for dipping. Served with one or two salads the whole spread will prove surprisingly substantial.*

If during the course of the meal the fondues become cold and too thick to dip into, return to microwave for a few seconds.

Serves 6

1 garlic clove, skinned and crushed
300 ml (½ pint) dry white wine
5 ml (1 tsp) lemon juice
100 g (4 oz) Brie
150 g (6 oz) mozzarella
300 g (10 oz) Gruyère, grated
15 ml (1 level tbsp) cornflour
30 ml (2 tbsp) kirsch
salt and freshly ground black pepper

1. Place garlic in a bowl with the wine and lemon juice. Cover and microwave on HIGH for 3 minutes until heated through.

2. Cut rind from the Brie and roughly cube. Dice the mozzarella. Add all the cheeses to the wine mixture. Cover and microwave on HIGH for 3 minutes, stirring once until the cheeses have melted.

3. Blend the cornflour with the kirsch and beat into the cheese mixture. Cover and microwave on HIGH for a further 2–2½ minutes until slightly thickened and smooth, whisking twice. (The mixture will thicken further while standing.)

4. Season to taste and leave to stand for 3 minutes. Divide among 6 individual warmed bowls and serve with fondue or ordinary forks, or with long wooden skewers.

———— COOK'S TIP ————
Mussels and clams can be cooked without any liquid, preserving maximum flavour. Place in a bowl, cover and microwave until opened.

See photograph page 44

MIXED FISH LASAGNE

Even microwaved lasagne is not particularly fast, but because the various fish are encased in layers of pasta, the resulting flavour and naturally moist texture is unbeatable.

Serves 4–5

30 ml (2 tbsp) oil
175 g (6 oz) lasagne verdi
1 large onion, peeled and chopped
2 sticks of celery, sliced
5 ml (1 level tsp) fresh chopped thyme or 2.5 ml ($\frac{1}{2}$ level tsp) dried
450 g (1 lb) cod or haddock fillet
225 g (8 oz) huss
100 g (4 oz) peeled prawns
300 ml ($\frac{1}{2}$ pint) Mushroom Sauce (see page 31)
salt and freshly ground pepper
50 g (2 oz) brown breadcrumbs
25 g (1 oz) ground almonds
a little butter or margarine

1. Place 15 ml (1 tbsp) of the oil in a bowl with 1.2 litres (2 pints) boiling water. Add lasagne one sheet at a time so that they do not stick together. Microwave on HIGH for 3 minutes then leave pasta in the water while preparing the filling.

2. Place the onion and celery in a bowl with the thyme and remaining oil. Cover and microwave on HIGH for 5 minutes until softened, stirring once.

3. Cut cod or haddock into chunks, discarding skin and bones. Cut huss into small chunks, discarding bone. Stir fish, prawns and 75 ml (5 level tbsp) of the Mushroom Sauce into onion mixture and season lightly.

4. Layer up fish mixture and pasta in a large shallow dish, finishing with a layer of fish. Spoon remaining sauce over fish and sprinkle with breadcrumbs and almonds.

5. Dot with butter or margarine. Cover and microwave on HIGH for 7 minutes. Remove cover and microwave on HIGH for a further 3 minutes. Cover and stand for 5 minutes.

BAKED MACKEREL WITH FOAMING ORANGE SAUCE

So common a sight at the fishmonger, we tend to take for granted this beautiful fish. Here it is served whole to show off the steely blue markings, with a foamy citrus sauce to counteract the extreme richness.

Serves 4

3 egg yolks
zest of 2 oranges
juice of 1 orange
10 ml (2 tsp) wine vinegar
2.5 ml ($\frac{1}{2}$ level tsp) sugar
4 small mackerel, cleaned and gutted
salt and freshly ground pepper

1. Place egg yolks, orange zest and juice, vinegar, sugar and seasoning into a bowl and reserve.

2. Make several cuts down each side of mackerel. Season inside and out and arrange on a plate. Cover and microwave on HIGH for 10 minutes, turning over half way through cooking. Cover and leave to stand while finishing the sauce.

3. Beat sauce with an electric whisk until well blended. Microwave on HIGH for 30 seconds. Beat for a further 3–4 minutes until thick and pale. Microwave on MEDIUM for a further 1 minute until heated through. Re-whisk lightly and pour a little over the mackerel.

4. Serve remainder in a separate sauceboat.

See photograph page 42–43

FRICASSÉ OF FISH

★ *Despite its flat shape John Dory can be difficult to fillet so if possible ask the fishmonger to do the job for you. John Dory, although delicious, can be equally difficult to buy but Dover or lemon sole, turbot or halibut make good substitutes.*

Serves 4

900 g (2 lb) John Dory fillets

30 ml (2 level tbsp) fresh chopped parsley or chervil

salt and freshly ground black pepper

2.5 ml (½ level tsp) cornflour

30 ml (2 tbsp) dry Vermouth

150 ml (¼ pint) double cream

Garnish

sprigs of parsley or chervil

1. Cut the fillets into thick strips and arrange in a single layer in a large shallow dish. Sprinkle with the parsley or chervil and a little seasoning.

2. Cover and microwave on HIGH for 5–6 minutes, carefully re-arranging the pieces of fish once during cooking. Drain the fish and transfer to a serving plate. Keep warm.

3. Blend the cornflour with the Vermouth and add to the juices in the dish. Stir in the cream.

4. Microwave on HIGH for 1 minute until heated through, stirring once. Season to taste and spoon over the fish. Serve garnished with parsley or chervil.

FRESH TUNA AND POTATO CASSEROLE

★ *One of the nicest fish dishes I had last year on holiday, was a simple tuna 'stew' with huge chunks of floury potato in a thick, rich gravy. This may seem a slightly mundane treatment for such a 'superior' sort of fish but the results are worthy of any special meal.*

Serves 4

450 g (1 lb) potatoes, peeled and cut into chunks

1 large onion, peeled and chopped

2–3 garlic cloves, skinned and crushed

1 stick of celery, sliced

15 ml (1 tbsp) olive oil

15 ml (1 level tbsp) plain flour

350 ml (12 fl oz) fish stock

15 ml (1 level tbsp) tomato purée

5 ml (1 tsp) anchovy essence

15 ml (1 level tbsp) fresh chopped coriander

salt and freshly ground black pepper

Garnish

chopped coriander or parsley

1. Place the potatoes in a shallow dish with 45 ml (3 tbsp) water. Cover and microwave on HIGH for 5 minutes, turning once, until the potatoes are just tender.

2. Place the onion in a large dish with the garlic, celery and oil. Cover and microwave on HIGH for 5 minutes, stirring once, until completely softened.

3. Stir in the flour and microwave on HIGH for 40 seconds. Gradually beat in the stock, tomato purée, anchovy essence, coriander and seasoning.

4. Toss the potatoes in the mixture then gently stir in the fish.

5. Cover and microwave on HIGH for 5 minutes until fish is cooked through, carefully stirring the ingredients once.

6. Leave to stand for 3 minutes. Serve sprinkled with chopped coriander or parsley.

PASTA IN PEPPERPOOL SAUCE

A sprinkling of turmeric transforms pasta into a vivid shade of yellow which is further emphasized by the contrasting puddle of pepper sauce. Combined with squid, celery, basil and tomatoes the flavour is distinctly Mediterranean.

Serves 4

5 ml (1 level tsp) ground turmeric
2 green chillies, halved
salt and freshly ground black pepper
275 g (10 oz) rigattoni pasta
1 red pepper
150 ml ($\frac{1}{4}$ pint) fish or vegetable stock or fish fumet
450–700 g (1–1$\frac{1}{2}$ lb) squid, cleaned
2.5 ml ($\frac{1}{2}$ tsp) olive oil
2.5 ml ($\frac{1}{2}$ level tsp) fresh chopped basil or 1.5 ml ($\frac{1}{4}$ level tsp) dried
4 tomatoes, cut into wedges
2 sticks of celery, cut into thin strips

To serve

Parmesan cheese (optional)

1. Place 1.2 litres (2 pints) boiling water in a bowl with the turmeric, chillies, salt and pasta. Microwave on HIGH for about 7 minutes, stirring once until almost tender. Leave to stand in the water.

2. Halve the red pepper, discarding stalk end and seeds. Microwave on HIGH for 2$\frac{1}{2}$–3 minutes until softened. Roughly chop, then blend in a liquidizer or food processor with the stock. Season lightly to taste.

3. Cut the squid into rings and thoroughly dry on kitchen paper. Place in a shallow dish with the oil and basil. Cover and microwave on HIGH for 1$\frac{1}{2}$ minutes stirring once. Add the tomatoes and celery and cook for 1 minute.

4. Cover the pepper sauce and microwave on HIGH for 1 minute until heated through. Spoon onto warmed serving plates.

5. Drain the pasta, reserving the chillies. Toss the pasta, chillies and squid mixture and season to taste.

6. Spoon over the pepper sauce and serve.

See photograph page 83

FAMILY FISH STEW

An everyday meal that is quickly combined in one bowl. To speed up preparation buy ready prepared squid and frozen stir-fry vegetables.

Serves 4

225 g (8 oz) squid
450 g (1 lb) cod or haddock fillet
15 ml (1 tbsp) oil
1 large leek, sliced
1 stick of celery, sliced
2 garlic cloves, crushed (optional)
30 ml (2 level tbsp) plain flour
300 ml (½ pint) milk
sachet of bouquet garni
600 ml (1 pint) clams or mussels

1. Cut squid into rings. Cut cod or haddock into chunks, discarding skin and bones.

2. Place oil, leek, celery and garlic if using, in a large bowl. Cover and microwave on HIGH for 3 minutes until softened.

3. Stir in flour then milk, bouquet garni, squid, cod or haddock. Cover and microwave on HIGH for 3 minutes, stirring once.

4. Add clams or mussels and cook on HIGH for a further 3 minutes until shellfish have opened. Return any unopened shellfish to microwave and cook on HIGH for a further 1 minute. Discard any which remain closed.

5. Cover and leave to stand for 3 minutes. Serve garnished with paprika.

See photograph page 42

SHREDDED SKATE SALAD WITH DEVILLED DRESSING

Skate has a unique way of falling off its cartilaginous wings into delicate threads of flesh that is marvellous in salads. Please do not shun cold fish dishes – besides the famous cold poached salmon – they are underrated and unexplored.

Serves 4

2 skate wings (about 700 g [1 ½ lb] in total weight)
2.5 ml (½ level tsp) ground paprika
salt
120 ml (8 tbsp) olive oil
30 ml (2 tbsp) wine vinegar
20 ml (4 tsp) Worcester sauce
10 ml (2 level tsp) English mustard
20 ml (4 tsp) tomato purée
salt and freshly ground black pepper
2 oranges
½ curley endive or crisp lettuce, shredded

1. Place the skate wings on a large plate. Add 15 ml (1 tbsp) water and sprinkle with the paprika and salt. Cover and microwave on HIGH for 7 minutes, turning once until cooked through. Leave to stand for 5 minutes.

2. Mix together the oil, vinegar, Worcester sauce, mustard, tomato purée and seasoning.

3. Cut rind from the oranges. Thinly slice the flesh, discarding any pips. Lay the curley endive or lettuce over 4 serving plates.

4. Using a fork shred skate away from bones and arrange over the endive or lettuce.

5. Top with orange slices and dressing.

——— SERVING SUGGESTION ———
A bowl of steaming new potatoes or Pilau Rice (page 120) would make this salad ample for four servings.

See photograph page 84

CHESTNUT STUFFED SOLE

Although there is little stomach cavity in flat fish the two upper most fillets can be rolled back attractively to contain a chosen stuffing. This recipe uses dried chestnuts from health food stores, which retain their deliciously nutty texture even after blending.

Serves 4

Stuffing

125 g (4.4 oz) packet dried chestnuts, soaked overnight

15 g (½ oz) butter or margarine

2 rashers streaky bacon, chopped

small handful of fresh parsley

2.5 ml (½ tsp) lemon juice

salt and freshly ground black pepper

4 small lemon or Dover sole

knob of butter or margarine

Garnish

lemon slices

parsley

1. Drain the soaked chestnuts and place in a bowl with 75 ml (3 fl oz) boiling water. Cover and microwave on HIGH for 5 minutes until softened, stirring once.

2. Place the butter or margarine and bacon in a separate bowl and microwave on HIGH for 1½ minutes.

3. Place the chestnuts and cooking juice in a liquidizer or food processor with the bacon and melted fat, parsley, lemon juice and seasoning. Blend until almost smooth.

4. Cut fins from fish and trim tail neatly. Place one sole on a board, dark skin side uppermost. Using a sharp knife make a cut from head to tail down the centre of the fish. Slip the knife under one fillet and cut the fish. Once fillet is removed enough, roll back slightly. Cut the other fillet away from the bone in the same way. Repeat with remaining fish.

5. Spread the chestnut stuffing down the exposed cavity, pressing down lightly. Dot fish with butter or margarine and season lightly.

6. Arrange two sole in the microwave. Cover with kitchen paper and microwave on HIGH for 3–4 minutes until just cooked through. Transfer to warmed serving plates while cooking remaining fish.

7. Place a knob of butter over stuffing and garnish fish with lemon and parsley.

See photograph page 101

TAGLIATELLE WITH BASIL AND CLAMS

This recipe can only be made with the delicate and dainty 'Venus' clams. Unfortunately they are infrequently available but do not be tempted to substitute the huge common clam (which is better suited to stuffings and chowder). Opt for mussels instead.

Serves 4

225 g (8 oz) tagliatelle verdi
1.2 litres (2 pints) clams, scrubbed
15 ml (1 level tbsp) fresh chopped basil, or 5 ml (1 level tsp) dried
600 ml (1 pint) Rich Tomato Sauce (see page 32)
salt and freshly ground black pepper

1. Place 1.2 litres (2 pints) boiling water in a bowl with the tagliatelle. Microwave on HIGH for 4–5 minutes until just tender. Leave to stand while preparing sauce.

2. Place clams in a large dish. Cover and microwave on HIGH for 4 minutes until clams have opened, stirring once.

3. Remove clams and return any unopened ones to microwave on HIGH for a further 1–2 minutes. Discard any which still remain closed.

4. Remove three quarters of the clams from their shells and add to the tomato sauce with the basil. Drain pasta and toss with the sauce and seasoning.

5. Top with unshelled clams. Cover and microwave on HIGH for a further 2–3 minutes until heated through.

Chestnut stuffed sole (page 99) and Leeks with yogurt dressing (page 116).

OVERLEAF

From the left clockwise: Bacon wrapped mullet (page 87); Cod steaks au poivre (page 93); Baked giant prawns with garlic dressing (page 48); Trio of smoked fish with melon sauce (page 53).

Stir-fried squid (page 51) and Chilli fish (page 74).

SEAFOOD PIZZA

Microwaves are excellent for proving dough, but less successful for browning bread. In a pizza however the problem does not arise as the pale crust is generously covered with a gooey cheese and seafood layer.

Serves 3–4

275 g (10 oz) packet white bread mix
30 ml (2 level tbsp) tomato purée
3–4 tomatoes, sliced
salt and freshly ground black pepper
2.5 ml ($\frac{1}{2}$ level tsp) fresh chopped basil or oregano, or 1.5 ml ($\frac{1}{4}$ level tsp) dried
100 g (4 oz) mozzarella or Cheddar cheese, thinly sliced
300 ml ($\frac{1}{2}$ pint) mussels or small clams
50 g (2 oz) cooked cockles
50 g (2–3 oz) peeled prawns

1. Make up bread mix following packet directions. After kneading place in a polythene bag and tie ends, trapping plenty of air inside. Microwave on HIGH for 15 seconds. Leave to stand for 10 minutes. Repeat twice more until dough has risen.

2. Roll out dough as thinly as possible on a floured surface and use to cover a lightly greased 25 cm (10 in) plate.

3. Spread dough to within 1 cm ($\frac{1}{2}$ in) of edges with tomato purée. Cover with sliced tomatoes. Season and sprinkle with basil or oregano. Top tomatoes with the cheese.

4. Arrange mussels or clams, cockles and prawns in a spiral over the cheese.

5. Cover loosely and microwave on HIGH for 12 minutes. Uncover and brush crust of pizza with some of the oozing juices from the filling. Microwave uncovered on HIGH for a further 2–3 minutes.

—— COOK'S TIP ——

After rolling the pizza base, dough trimmings can be shaped into rolls, baked in the microwave and popped under the grill to lightly brown.

See photograph page 84

PAELLA

The appeal of Paella lies in the fact that the fish can be varied to suit your mood – and your pocket! Squid and prawns are perfectly adequate for family meals but Dublin Bay or King prawns, crayfish tails, mussels or clams can be added for a taste of the 'exotic'. The saffron is vital for an authentic taste, as is Spanish or Italian rice, usually labelled 'risotto rice' at the supermarket.

Serves 4–6

6 chicken thighs
1 onion, peeled and chopped
3 garlic cloves, skinned and crushed
45 ml (3 tbsp) olive oil
5 ml (1 level tsp) ground paprika
225 g (8 oz) risotto rice
about 20 saffron strands, crushed and soaked overnight in 30 ml (2 tbsp) boiling water
4 tomatoes, skinned and chopped
450 ml (¾ pint) hot chicken or fish stock
1 red pepper, sliced
30 ml (2 tbsp) fresh chopped parsley
50 g (2 oz) frozen peas
225 g (8 oz) squid, cleaned
225 g (8 oz) small whole prawns
600 ml (1 pint) mussels, cockles or clams, scrubbed
6 crayfish tails, Dublin Bay or King prawns (optional)
salt and freshly ground black pepper

1. Pierce the chicken thighs with a fork. Place in a large dish with the onion and garlic. Brush with the oil and sprinkle with paprika. Cover and microwave on HIGH for 5 minutes, re-arranging the chicken once.

2. Stir in the rice and microwave on HIGH for 1 minute. Add the saffron, tomatoes and stock. Cover and microwave on HIGH for 10 minutes until rice is tender, stirring twice.

3. Stir in the red pepper, parsley, peas, squid and small prawns.

4. Spread the mussels, cockles or clams over the surface along with the crayfish tails, Dublin Bay or King prawns if using. Season generously.

5. Cover and microwave on HIGH for a further 3 minutes until mussels, cockles or clams have opened. Remove any which have not opened and microwave these on HIGH for a further 1 minute. Discard any which still remain closed.

6. Leave to stand for 3 minutes before serving.

MOUCLADE OF MUSSELS

Only fractionally more involved than the classic Moules à la Marinière, this creamy aniseed 'Mouclade' makes a superb starter for four (or luxurious meal for two). Add seasoning with care, the mussel juices are naturally very salty.

Serves 2

25 g (1 oz) butter

4 shallots, peeled and finely chopped

1–2 garlic cloves, skinned and crushed

½ small fennel bulb, sliced

5 ml (1 level tsp) plain flour

120 ml (4 fl oz) dry white wine

15 ml (1 tbsp) Pernod

900 g (2 lb) mussels, scrubbed

150 ml (¼ pint) double cream

salt and freshly ground black pepper

To serve

crusty bread

1. Place the butter in a large bowl and microwave on HIGH for 1 minute until melted. Add the shallots, garlic and fennel. Cover and microwave on HIGH for 2½–3 minutes until the fennel has softened.

2. Stir in the flour then gradually blend in the wine and Pernod.

3. Add the mussels, cover and microwave on HIGH for 4 minutes. Remove any mussels which have not opened and return to the microwave on HIGH for a further 1 minute. Discard any which still remain closed.

4. Stir in the cream and season lightly. Return to the microwave on HIGH for a further 1 minute until reheated. Serve immediately with crusty bread.

See cover photograph

CRAB CRÉOLE

Luxurious, yet affordable crab, blends particularly well with spicy flavours. Use frozen crabmeat, not canned, or better still, prepare a whole fresh crab, instructions for which are on page 28.

Serves 3–4

1 onion, peeled and chopped

10 ml (2 tsp) oil

1.5 ml (¼ level tsp) curry paste

1.5 ml (¼ level tsp) mild chilli powder

1 garlic clove, skinned and unshed

227 g (8 oz) can chopped tomatoes

25 g (1 oz) creamed coconut

10 ml (2 tsp) lime or lemon juice

75 ml (3 fl oz) pineapple juice

700 g (1½ lb) whole crab, prepared, or 225 g (8 oz) crabmeat

salt and freshly ground black pepper

1. Place the onion in a large dish with the oil, curry paste, chilli powder and garlic. Cover and microwave on HIGH for 3 minutes, stirring once.

2. Stir in the tomatoes, coconut, lime or lemon juice, pineapple juice, crabmeat and seasoning.

3. Cover and microwave on HIGH for a further 3 minutes stirring twice, until thickened and heated through.

4. Leave to stand for 3 minutes.

SERVING SUGGESTION

If using fresh crab, clean out the shells and use as an attractive serving container. Any remaining sauce can be served in a sauceboat.

RICH SHELLFISH MOUSSE

★ *This makes a lovely summer lunch party dish with new potatoes and a crisp vegetable or tossed salad. Like most cold mousses, little cooking is required but the gentle poaching of the scallops and the simple method of dissolving gelatine makes it worthy of the microwave treatment.*

Serves 6

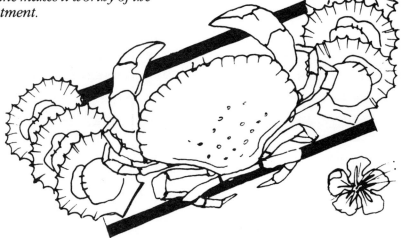

| 225 g (8 oz) scallops |
| salt and freshly ground black pepper |
| 450 ml (¾ pint) fish stock or fish fumet |
| 350 g (12 oz) whole prawns, peeled |
| 225 g (8 oz) brown and white crabmeat |
| 15 ml (1 level tbsp) powdered gelatine |
| 300 ml (½ pint) double cream |

1. Place the scallops in a shallow dish with a little seasoning. Cover and microwave on HIGH for 1–1½ minutes until just cooked. Place in a liquidizer or food processor with 150 ml (¼ pint) of the fish stock and the peeled prawns. Blend until smooth and turn into a bowl.

2. Blend the crabmeat with another 150 ml (¼ pint) of the stock and turn into a separate bowl.

3. Sprinkle the gelatine over the remaining 150 ml (¼ pint) of the stock and leave for 5 minutes. Cover and microwave on HIGH for 1 minute or until the gelatine has dissolved. Beat half the gelatine into the scallop purée and remaining half into the crab purée.

4. When the mixtures are on the point of setting, whip the cream until peaking. Divide evenly between the two bowls and fold in with a metal spoon.

5. Spoon the crab mixture into 6 lightly oiled cups or large ramekin dishes.

6. Immediately spoon the scallop mixture into the centres of each so that it becomes enveloped by the crab mixtures. Place in the refrigerator for at least 2 hours until set.

7. To serve, loosen edges of mousses with a knife. Dip into boiling water for a few seconds then invert onto serving plates.

SERVING SUGGESTION
Dipping mousses in hot water for too long when turning out can easily result in disappointing, over softened results. A more time consuming but safer method is to invert the ramekin onto the serving plate and cover with a very hot cloth until the mousse loosens itself from the mould.

See photograph page 64

FLAMBÉED LOBSTER WITH CREAM

★ *Having selected your perfect lobster and cooked it yourself, (see page 14), or had the fishmonger cook it for you, here is a recipe that will do it justice. A larger lobster will provide more servings but the flavour seems to deteriorate with size.*

Serves 2

700 g (1½ lb) whole cooked lobster
25 g (1 oz) butter
½ small onion, peeled and finely chopped
30 ml (2 tbsp) brandy
50 ml (2 fl oz) dry white wine
45 ml (3 tbsp) double cream
good pinch of cayenne pepper
5 ml (1 level tsp) tomato purée
salt and freshly ground black pepper

1. Prepare the lobster. Twist off the claws and legs using a hammer or rolling pin, break open the claws and scoop out the flesh. Using a sharp knife cut the lobster in half lengthways and pull apart into equal halves.

2. Pull and discard the cartilaginous stomach sac from near the head. Pull out the thread-like intestinal canal which runs down the length of the tail.

3. Remove all the meat from the lobster and roughly cut into pieces.

4. Place the butter in a flameproof dish and microwave on HIGH until melted. Add the onion, cover and microwave on HIGH for 2 minutes until softened.

5. Add the lobster meat and microwave on HIGH for 1 minute. Remove from the microwave. Stir in the brandy and immediately light with a taper. When the flames die down drain the lobster and return to the shells.

6. Stir the wine, cream, cayenne, tomato purée and seasoning into the pan juices. Season lightly to taste.

7. Spoon the cream mixture over the lobster. Microwave on HIGH for a further 1–2 minutes until heated through.

——— COOK'S TIP ———
Female lobster contain a rich pink roe or 'coral'. If present, remove from the lobster after cutting in half, and add to the sauce with the cream.

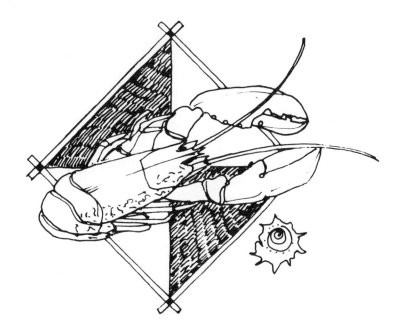

FISH CASSOULET

Like the traditional meat cassoulet this faster variation has a thick, buttery breadcrumb 'crust'. To improve its colour, pop under the grill just before serving.

Serves 6

450 g (1 lb) smoked haddock or cod fillet

150 ml (¼ pint) fish stock or fish fumet

1 onion, peeled and sliced

100 g (4 oz) smoked streaky bacon, roughly chopped

50 g (2 oz) coarse garlic sausages, chopped

397 g (14 oz) can red kidney beans

397 g (14 oz) can baked beans

salt and freshly ground black pepper

2 bay leaves

25 g (1 oz) butter or margarine

50 g (2 oz) breadcrumbs

1. Place the fish in a shallow dish with 30 ml (2 tbsp) of the stock. Cover and microwave on HIGH for 4 minutes until barely cooked. Drain fish, reserving liquid and roughly flake the flesh discarding skin and bones.

2. Place the onion and bacon in a large dish. Cover and microwave on HIGH for 2 minutes, stirring once until the onion has softened. Stir in the sausages, red kidney beans and baked beans, remaining stock, seasoning and bay leaves. Carefully fold in the fish.

3. Melt the butter or margarine on HIGH for 1 minute. Stir in the breadcrumbs and spoon over the cassoulet, pressing down lightly.

4. Cover with kitchen paper and microwave on HIGH for 5 minutes until fish is heated through. Uncover and microwave on HIGH for a further 2 minutes. Leave to stand for 3 minutes before serving.

See photograph page 83

STORECUPBOARD HASH

Once again, canned fish comes to the rescue for a speedy family meal. Virtually any fish can be made use of here, except perhaps canned crab which is best reserved for salads and sandwiches – if used at all!

Serves 3–4

450 g (1 lb) potatoes, peeled and diced

15 ml (1 tbsp) oil

salt and freshly ground black pepper

2.5 ml (½ level tsp) ground paprika

1 onion, peeled and chopped

1 carrot, peeled and grated

1 stick of celery, finely sliced

2.5 ml (½ level tsp) fennel seeds (optional)

approx. 200 g (7 oz) canned fish in brine

30 ml (2 level tbsp) tomato ketchup

25 g (1 oz) Cheddar cheese, grated

1. Toss the potatoes in a shallow dish with 5 ml (1 tsp) of the oil, salt and paprika. Cover and microwave on HIGH for 5 minutes, stirring once, until tender.

2. Place the onion, carrot, celery, fennel if using, and remaining oil in a separate dish. Cover and microwave on HIGH for 2½ minutes, stirring once.

3. Stir in the drained fish, ketchup and seasoning. Cover with the prepared potatoes and press down lightly.

4. Sprinkle the surface with the grated cheese and microwave on HIGH for a further 1–2 minutes until heated through and the cheese has melted.

SMOKED FISH KEBABS

Enveloped in bacon rolls, cubes of fish stay deliciously moist and succulent, and you can be well assured that they are perfectly cooked just as the bacon is ready. Long wooden kebab skewers, available from good kitchen stores, must be substituted for metal ones.

Serves 4

350 g (12 oz) smoked haddock fillets

225 g (8 oz) courgettes

7 long rashers streaky bacon

30–45 ml (2–3 level tbsp) creamed horseradish

15 g ($\frac{1}{2}$ oz) butter or margarine

To serve

300 ml ($\frac{1}{2}$ pint) Cheese Sauce (see page 31)

1. Cut haddock fillets into about 20 chunks, discarding any skin and bones.

2. Cut courgettes diagonally into 1 cm ($\frac{1}{2}$ in) slices.

3. Stretch bacon rashers with the back of a knife, then cut each into three.

4. Spread horseradish over bacon. Roll a piece of fish in each piece of bacon. Alternate fish and bacon on 4 wooden skewers with the courgettes. Arrange on a flat plate.

5. Melt butter or margarine on HIGH for 30 seconds. Brush over kebabs and cover loosely with kitchen paper.

6. Microwave on HIGH for 8–10 minutes re-arranging kebabs once during cooking.

7. Whisk any cooking juices in to the Cheese Sauce and reheat on HIGH for 1–2 minutes. Serve with the kebabs.

—— COOK'S TIP ——
Other cheaper fish work well in this recipe. Try smoked whiting or unsmoked coley.

See photograph page 62

TUNA AND EGG BAKES

Eggs baked in a nest of broccoli and tuna make an easy lunch with crusty breads, or more satisfying family meal with jacket-baked potatoes.

Serves 4

225 g (8 oz) broccoli, trimmed

354 g (12 oz) can tuna in brine

300 ml ($\frac{1}{2}$ pint) Mushroom or Cheese Sauce (see page 31)

salt and freshly ground black pepper

4 eggs

1. Place the broccoli in a shallow dish with 45 ml (3 tbsp) water. Cover and microwave on HIGH for 4–5 minutes until almost tender. Drain and cut broccoli into short lengths.

2. Drain and roughly flake the tuna. Arrange with the broccoli around the edges of 4 cereal bowls leaving a well in the centres of the bowls. Season lightly.

3. Spoon the sauce over the broccoli and tuna, and break an egg into the centre of each bowl. Season the eggs lightly.

4. Cover each dish and microwave on HIGH for 7–9 minutes until eggs are lightly set. Leave to stand for 3 minutes.

—— COOK'S TIP ——
If your cereal bowls are very wide and do not all fit in the microwave together cook two at a time, allowing 4–5 minutes on HIGH.

FISH RISOTTO WITH SPICY PEANUT SAUCE

Microwaved rice does not cook exceptionally fast but neither does it turn 'stodgy', even if slightly overcooked. Here, brown rice provides the basis of a semi-storecupboard risotto that only requires the simplest leafy salad accompaniment.

Serves 4

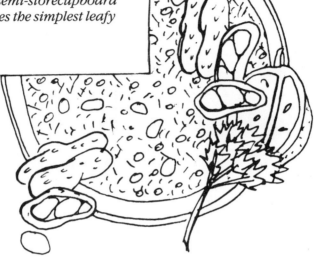

1 leek, sliced
2 sticks of celery, sliced
10 ml (2 tsp) oil
225 g (8 oz) brown rice
600 ml (1 pint) hot fish stock
salt and freshly ground black pepper
1 red pepper, diced
212 g (7½ oz) can red salmon

Sauce

45 ml (3 level tbsp) smooth peanut butter
1 garlic clove, crushed
25 g (1 oz) creamed coconut
150 ml (¼ pint) orange juice
2.5 ml (½ level tsp) mild chilli powder
10 ml (2 tsp) soy sauce

1. Place the leek, celery and oil in a shallow dish. Cover and microwave on HIGH for 1 minute. Stir in rice and cook on HIGH for a further 1 minute.

2. Stir in the stock and seasoning. Cover and microwave on HIGH for 20 minutes, stirring twice until the rice is just tender.

3. Meanwhile combine the peanut butter, garlic, creamed coconut, orange juice, chilli powder and soy sauce in a bowl.

4. Once the rice is cooked stir in the red pepper, drained salmon and seasoning. Microwave on HIGH for a further 2 minutes until heated through. Cover and leave to stand while cooking sauce.

5. Cover bowl of sauce and microwave on HIGH for 3–4 minutes, stirring frequently until smooth. Season to taste and serve with the risotto.

—— COOK'S TIP ——
Peanut sauces have a tendancy to suddenly 'over' thicken. If this happens stir in a little more orange juice.

SARDINE STUFFED PASTA SHELLS

This recipe may seem a little extravagant on the sardines but at the price per can it still makes a very cheap meal. Use only the very large pasta shells (the smaller ones are too time consuming to stuff) and serve with a crisply cooked vegetable or salad.

Serves 4

225 g (8 oz) pasta shells
½ small onion, peeled and grated
40 g (1½ oz) breadcrumbs
3 × 120 g (4½ oz) cans sardines in oil or brine
45 ml (3 level tbsp) tomato relish
30 ml (2 tbsp) fresh chopped parsley
salt and freshly ground black pepper

Dressing

150 ml (¼ pint) Greek strained yogurt
grated zest and juice of 1 lemon
15 ml (1 level tbsp) mayonnaise

1. Place the pasta shells in a large bowl with 1.2 litres (2 pints) boiling water. Microwave on HIGH for 5 minutes or until almost tender. Drain.

2. Beat together the onion, breadcrumbs, drained sardines, relish, parsley and seasoning. Spoon the mixture into the pasta shells and arrange on a large plate.

3. Beat together the yogurt, lemon zest and juice, mayonnaise and seasoning.

4. Cover the prepared shells and microwave on HIGH for 2 minutes until heated through, carefully stirring once.

5. Serve with the dressing spooned over.

SMOKED FISH WITH MUSTARD AND TARRAGON

This recipe is designed for whole hot-smoked fish which, although ready for eating cold, benefit from a brief heating in the microwave to bring out their flavours. Try Arbroath smokies, buckling and if you can get them, tiny whole smoked mackerel.

Serves 4

4 small hot-smoked fish, heads removed
4 small sprigs of oregano
small knob of butter
60 ml (4 tbsp) garlic or white wine vinegar
grated zest of ½ lemon or 1 lime
salt and freshly ground black pepper

1. If using buckling, gut the fish first. Score the fish down each side with a sharp knife and arrange on a large flat plate. Place a sprig of oregano into the cavity of each fish.

2. Place the butter in a small bowl and microwave on HIGH for about 30 seconds until melted. Stir in the vinegar, lemon or lime zest and seasoning. Spoon over the fish.

3. Cover loosely and microwave on HIGH for 1 minute until warmed through. Transfer to serving plates and spoon the juices over.

4. Serve with brown bread and butter.

—— COOK'S TIP ——
Dried oregano can be substituted for the fresh, although the results will not be so aromatic.

MACKEREL AND MUSHROOM BURGERS

I have called these 'burgers' rather than fishcakes as they lack the careful 'patting and shaping' of the latter. Designed as homemade 'fast food', the fish is canned and the potatoes unpeeled – which all makes for wonderfully easy, but tasty results. Why not serve gherkins, relishes and commercial 'microchips' to complete the feast.

Serves 4

350 g (12 oz) potatoes
45 ml (3 tbsp) milk
45 ml (3 level tbsp) fresh chopped parsley
100 g (4 oz) mushrooms, finely chopped
2 × 125 g (4.4 oz) cans mackerel in brine, drained
5 ml (1 tsp) anchovy essence
salt and freshly ground black pepper
15 ml (1 tbsp) oil

1. Scrub and cut the potatoes into small chunks. Place in a shallow dish with the milk. Cover and microwave on HIGH for 4 minutes until potatoes are tender, stirring once.

2. Mash well and beat in the parsley, mushrooms, mackerel, anchovy essence and plenty of seasoning. Shape roughly into 4 'burgers' using well floured hands.

3. Preheat a browning dish following manufacturer's directions. Add oil and burgers and leave until sizzling dies down.

4. Turn burgers over. Cover and microwave on HIGH for 3 minutes. Leave to stand for 3 minutes.

SIDE
DISHES

LEEKS WITH YOGURT DRESSING

The great bonus of microwaving accompaniments is that you can cook them in their serving dishes (provided that the dishes do not have metallic rims) and dispense with washing up pans.

Leeks make a superb vegetable side dish when you tire of the more predictable ones. Sautéeing in butter accentuates their beautiful green colouring.

Serves 5–6

150 ml (¼ pint) natural yogurt
30 ml (2 level tbsp) mayonnaise
1.5 ml (¼ level tsp) English Mustard
salt and freshly ground black pepper
25 g (1 oz) butter
450 g (1 lb) leeks, trimmed and thinly sliced

Garnish

ground nutmeg

1. Blend together the yogurt, mayonnaise, mustard and seasoning.

2. Place the butter in a shallow dish and microwave on HIGH for 1 minute until melted. Stir in leeks until coated in the butter.

3. Cover and microwave on HIGH for 1–2 minutes, stirring once until softened but still holding their shape.

4. Spoon the dressing over the leeks and sprinkle with nutmeg.

See photograph page 101

RATATOUILLE

A wonderfully garlicky dish that blends particularly well with white fish. Highly adaptable, it can be served hot or cold, and any left overs, sprinkled with stringy cheese and reheated make a marvellous lunch dish with plenty of crusty bread and chilled wine.

Serves 4–6

225 g (8 oz) aubergine
salt and freshly ground black pepper
1 onion, peeled and sliced
2 garlic cloves, skinned and crushed
30 ml (2 tbsp) olive oil
450 g (1 lb) courgettes, trimmed and sliced diagonally
397 g (14 oz) can chopped tomatoes
30 ml (2 level tbsp) tomato purée
1.5 ml (¼ level tsp) caster sugar
1 red or yellow pepper, sliced
15 ml (1 level tbsp) fresh chopped parsley

1. Slice the aubergine and layer up in a colander, sprinkling each layer with plenty of salt. Leave for 30 minutes then rinse under cold running water. Drain on kitchen paper.

2. Place the onion, garlic and oil in a large shallow dish. Cover and microwave on HIGH for 3 minutes, stirring once. Add the aubergine slices and microwave on HIGH for 1½ minutes.

3. Stir in the courgettes, tomatoes, tomato purée, sugar and seasoning. Cover and microwave on HIGH for 3 minutes, stirring once.

4. Stir in the red or yellow pepper and parsley and season to taste. Cover and microwave on HIGH for a further 2 minutes. Leave to stand for 3 minutes.

STIR-FRIED COURGETTES AND MUSHROOMS

Combining two vegetables in one dish gives the impression of dedicated preparation. In fact this colourful accompaniment could not be simpler and does away with the need for an additional vegetable. Pine kernals, from the glossy cones of pine trees, make an interesting finishing touch, but substitute cashews or peanuts, if necessary, as pine kernals can be hard to come by.

Serves 4–6

450 g (1 lb) courgettes

15 ml (1 tbsp) oil

225 g (8 oz) button mushrooms, halved if large

salt and freshly ground black pepper

30 ml (2 level tbsp) pine kernals

1. Trim and cut the courgettes diagonally into slices.

2. Preheat a browning dish following manufacturer's directions. Add the oil and courgettes and stir until sizzling dies down.

3. Stir in the mushrooms. Cover and microwave on HIGH for 2–3 minutes, stirring once until the vegetables are softened to your liking.

4. Season lightly and serve sprinkled with pine kernals.

—— SERVING SUGGESTION ——
Delicious with most 'smart' fish dishes, especially salmon. Most browning dishes conveniently double up as serving containers but do make sure you use a sturdy table mat for protection as they generate a lot of heat.

See photograph page 81

SESAME BEANS AND BACON

Broad beans make a useful freezer standby to be brought out when the fresh offering of greens look uninviting. Serve with fish stews, pies and any tomato-based fish dishes.

Serves 4–6

2 rashers of streaky bacon, roughly diced

15 ml (1 tbsp) sesame or vegetable oil

15 ml (1 level tbsp) sesame seeds

350 g (12 oz) frozen broad beans

salt and freshly ground black pepper

1. Place the bacon in a shallow dish with the oil and sesame seeds. Cover and microwave on HIGH for 2 minutes, stirring once.

2. Stir in the broad beans and seasoning. Cover and microwave on HIGH for 5 minutes, stirring once until the beans are tender.

SCALLOP SHELL POTATOES

To continue the 'fish' theme, empty scallop shells (left over from a scallop recipe or bought from a good kitchen store) make attractive cases for plain mashed potato. Make ahead and heat through before serving.

Serves 6

700 g (1½ lb) potatoes, peeled and cut into chunks
salt and freshly ground black pepper
2 egg yolks
25 g (1 oz) butter
30 ml (2 tbsp) milk
30 ml (2 level tbsp) Parmesan cheese

1. Place potatoes in a shallow dish. Sprinkle with salt and add 45 ml (3 tbsp) water. Cover and microwave on HIGH for 8 minutes until potatoes are tender, stirring twice.

2. Mash potatoes with the egg yolks and butter until smooth. Stir in seasoning and milk.

3. Place in a piping bag fitted with a large star nozzle and pipe rosettes into six cleaned scallop shells. Sprinkle with Parmesan cheese.

4. Arrange in the microwave (you may need to overlap shells slightly) and cover loosely with kitchen paper. Microwave on HIGH for 3–4 minutes until hot.

SHREDDED POTATO BAKE

This golden 'cake' of potato is the nearest you can get, successfully, to fried potatoes in the microwave. Soaking the potatoes in water is not vital but will remove any 'starchiness' that might otherwise make the finished dish rather heavy.

Serves 4

450 g (1 lb) potatoes
1 small onion, finely chopped
30 ml (2 level tbsp) fresh chopped parsley
salt and freshly ground black pepper
15 g (½ oz) butter
15 ml (1 tbsp) oil

Garnish

extra chopped parsley

1. Peel and coarsely grate the potatoes. Place in a bowl of water and leave to soak for 2 hours.

2. Thoroughly drain the potatoes and pat dry between two clean tea towels. Mix together with the onion, parsley and plenty of seasoning.

3. Preheat a browning dish following manufacturer's directions. Add the butter and oil, then quickly pack the shredded potato mixture into the dish. Microwave on HIGH for 2 minutes.

4. Turn over the potatoes. (This is easiest done by inverting them out onto a plate and then sliding them back into the dish.) Cook on HIGH for a further 3 minutes.

5. Serve sprinkled with parsley.

MINTED POTATO CASTLES

Once turned out these prettily layered potatoes look as though you have laboured meticulously over their careful arrangement. Flavoured with mint and cream they make a perfect side dish to any delicate fish.

Serves 6

700 g (1½ b) new potatoes
salt and freshly ground black pepper
knob of butter
90 ml (6 tbsp) single cream
15 ml (1 level tbsp) finely chopped fresh mint
good pinch of ground nutmeg

1. Wash potatoes and scrape if liked. Place in a shallow dish with 45 ml (3 tbsp) water and a little salt. Cover and microwave on HIGH for 5 minutes, turning once until potatoes have softened. Leave to cool slightly.

2. Slice the potatoes as thinly as possible and layer up in 6 lightly buttered microwave ramekins.

3. Mix together the cream, mint, nutmeg, seasoning and 30 ml (2 tbsp) water. Spoon over the potatoes.

4. Cover the dishes and arrange in a circle, spaced slightly apart, in the microwave. Microwave on HIGH for 5–6 minutes, turning dishes once until the potatoes are tender.

5. Leave to stand for 3 minutes, then invert onto warmed serving plates.

HOT TOSSED BEETROOT

Tastier than the vinegary processed beetroot, and more convenient than the lengthy procedure of boiling the raw, is this unusual alternative – grated raw beetroot, tossed in butter and quickly flashed in the microwave.

Serves 4

450 g (1 lb) raw beetroot, skinned
25 g (1 oz) butter
salt and freshly ground black pepper
5 ml (1 level tsp) caraway or fennel seeds, crushed (optional)

1. Coarsely grate the beetroot using a food processor, electric mixer attachment, or by hand.

2. Place the butter in a shallow serving dish. Microwave on HIGH for 1 minute until melted. Add the beetroot and microwave on HIGH for 1 minute, stirring twice until the beetroot is heated through but not softened.

3. Season with salt and pepper and serve sprinkled with caraway or fennel seeds if liked.

SERVING SUGGESTION
Use to add 'bite' to oily fish dishes, particularly those using herrings and smoked fish. A spoonful of soured cream over the beetroot makes a nice finishing touch.

PILAU RICE

Rice that is served with fish is invariably plain boiled, but unless the dish is excessively rich, or delicate, I prefer a tastier 'pilau' which adds more colour and interest. If liked, omit the cinnamon and allspice for a gentler 'nutty' flavour.

Serves 4

1 onion, peeled and chopped

1 garlic clove, skinned and crushed (optional)

1 stick cinnamon, broken into 2 pieces

1.5 ml ($\frac{1}{4}$ level tsp) ground allspice

15 ml (1 tbsp) oil

225 g (8 oz) long grain brown rice

2.5 ml ($\frac{1}{2}$ level tsp) lightly crushed saffron strands, dissolved overnight in 15 ml (1 tbsp) boiling water, or 1.5 ml ($\frac{1}{4}$ level tsp) ground turmeric

50 g (2 oz) flaked almonds

salt and freshly ground black pepper

15 ml (1 level tbsp) fresh chopped coriander or parsley

1. Place the onion, garlic, if using, cinnamon stick and allspice in a shallow dish with the oil. Cover and microwave on HIGH for 3 minutes until onion has softened, stirring once.

2. Stir in the rice and microwave on HIGH for 1 minute.

3. Add the saffron or turmeric, almonds, seasoning and 450 ml (15 fl oz) hot water. Cover and microwave on HIGH for 15–20 minutes until rice is tender, stirring twice.

4. Stir in the coriander and leave to stand for 3 minutes.

CLAM SALAD

The plainest most uninteresting side salad can be transformed into something special with a garnish of small clams, or failing that mussels.

Serves 4

Dressing

60 ml (4 tbsp) olive oil

15 ml (1 tbsp) white wine or garlic vinegar

10 ml (2 level tsp) creamed horseradish

1.5 ml ($\frac{1}{4}$ level tsp) caster sugar

salt and freshly ground black pepper

300 ml ($\frac{1}{2}$ pint) Venus clams, cleaned

1 small lettuce

$\frac{1}{4}$ cucumber, sliced

3 tomatoes, cut into wedges

1. To make the dressing, place the oil, vinegar, horseradish, sugar and seasoning in a bowl and whisk well until combined.

2. Place the clams in a large bowl. Cover and microwave on HIGH for 2–3 minutes until the clams have opened. Return any which have not opened to the microwave and cook on HIGH for a further 1 minute. Discard any which still remain closed.

3. Arrange the lettuce, cucumber and tomatoes in a salad bowl and toss in the dressing. Top with the clams, still in their shells.

See photograph page 84

WARM SPINACH SALAD

Although most warm salads are pretty cold by the time they have gone from oven to table, and table to plate, heating them brings out and 'mingles' the various flavours.

Serves 6

225 g (8 oz) fresh spinach leaves

2 oranges, skinned and sliced

1 avocado, peeled and cut into chunks

50 g (2 oz) streaky bacon, finely chopped

30 ml (2 tbsp) walnut or olive oil

30 ml (2 tbsp) white wine vinegar

salt and freshly ground black pepper

1. Remove tough stalks from the spinach. Wash the spinach, breaking up any large leaves. Drain and pat dry on kitchen paper.

2. Place spinach in a microwave serving dish with the oranges and avocado. Microwave on MEDIUM for 1 minute, stirring once until warmed through but retaining firm texture. Cover and leave to stand.

3. Place the bacon in a small bowl with the oil. Cover with kitchen paper and microwave on HIGH for 1 minute. Stir in the vinegar and microwave on HIGH for a further 30 seconds.

3. Pour mixture over the salad and toss well with plenty of seasoning. Serve immediately.

—— COOK'S TIP ——
Watch closely as the spinach salad is warmed. The microwaving time will depend on the temperature of the ingredients on entering the oven, and over-cooking will produce limp results.

See photograph page 44

FENNEL SALAD WITH BEL PAESE DRESSING

When you fancy a change from the more usual vineagrette dressing try this delicately flavoured alternative, made using the individual foil-wrapped packs of Bel Paese cheese.

Serves 4

Dressing

2 × 28 g (1 oz) packets Bel Paese

45 ml (3 tbsp) milk

salt and freshly ground black pepper

2.5 ml ($\frac{1}{2}$ tsp) white wine vinegar

1 small fennel bulb

1 small lettuce

few sprigs of fennel or dill (optional)

1. To make the dressing place the Bel Paese in a bowl. Beat with an electric whisk until softened. Gradually add the milk, beating well until smooth. Season lightly and stir in the vinegar.

2. Trim and thinly slice the fennel. Arrange in a salad bowl with the lettuce and fennel or dill, if using. Serve the dressing separately.

See photograph page 43

CHERRY TOMATO SALAD

As pretty as they are the availability of cherry tomatoes cannot be relied on. As an alternative, slice 4 ordinary tomatoes into a dish. Pour over the dressing and microwave in the same way.

Serves 4

2 spring onions, trimmed and finely chopped

15 ml (1 tbsp) garlic or wine vinegar

30 ml (2 tbsp) olive oil

2.5 ml ($\frac{1}{2}$ level tsp) fresh chopped basil or a good pinch of dried

salt and freshly ground black pepper

12–18 cherry tomatoes, depending on size

Garnish

basil leaves

1. Mix spring onions with the vinegar, oil, basil and seasoning. Spoon onto a serving plate.

2. Cut a thin slice off the stalk ends of tomatoes and place cut sides down on plate. Cut a small cross on the top of each tomato and leave to marinate for 1–2 hours.

3. Cover with kitchen paper and microwave on HIGH for 1$\frac{1}{2}$–2 minutes until warmed through.

4. Serve garnished with basil leaves.

—— SERVING SUGGESTION ——
Deliciously sweet cherry tomatoes make a colourful accompaniment to any cold fish dishes or 'dry cooked' ones such as Stargazy Crumble (page 71) and Red Mullet en Papillote (page 72).

See photograph page 61

GARLIC AND HERB ROLLS

Do not be disappointed when the crusty-topped rolls you put into the microwave emerge rather 'limp'. They will return to their crusty state before you start eating.

Makes 4

4 small crusty rolls, round or long
50 g (2 oz) butter, softened
1–2 garlic cloves, skinned and crushed
10 ml (2 level tsp) fresh chopped mixed herbs or 2.5 ml (½ level tsp) dried
salt and freshly ground black pepper

1. Make several cuts, 1 cm (½ in) apart across the rolls, almost through to the base.

2. Beat the butter in a bowl with the garlic, herbs and seasoning. Spread the mixture into the cuts made in the rolls.

3. Arrange rolls spaced well apart in the microwave. Microwave on HIGH for 1 minute. Leave to stand for 3 minutes.

—— SERVING SUGGESTION ——
Equally as mouthwatering as garlic bread, these small rolls make daintier 'complete' servings. If liked, have ready some crumpled foil cases to serve the rolls in.

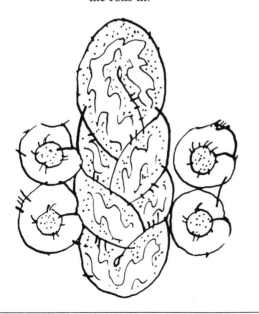

ROUILLE

Fierce and fiery Rouille is the classic way to 'hot' up fish soups and stews, the desired amount of which is swirled into the dish at the table. (Be cautious at first and add a scant spoonful!) For those who can take the heat, Rouille also makes an exciting dipping sauce for fritters and shellfish.

Serves 6

2 red chillies
2 garlic cloves, skinned and crushed
50 g (2 oz) crustless white bread steeped in milk and squeezed dry
60 ml (4 tbsp) olive oil
salt
75 ml (3 fl oz) fish stock or fish fumet

1. Halve the chillies and remove the seeds and stalk ends. Chop finely and place in a bowl with the garlic.

2. Add the bread to the bowl and beat well. Gradually beat in the oil until thick then beat in the fish stock. Season with a little salt.

3. Transfer to a small bowl and refrigerate, tightly sealed, until required.

—— COOK'S TIP ——
A smoother result can be obtained by making Rouille, mayonnaise style, in a liquidizer. Blend together the chillies, garlic and bread and then gradually add the oil in a steady stream until thickened. Add the stock in the same way.

GREEK YOGURT

In some of the preceding recipes I have recommended the irresistibly thick and creamy Greek-style yogurt as it gives a richer, smoother flavour than the ordinary. Homemade is not necessarily any tastier but may save you trudging around the shops looking for the bought version. If you are anything like me, make plenty as you may find it difficult to resist a spoonful each time you pass the fridge!

Makes 600 ml (1 pint)

---

600 ml (1 pint) natural yogurt

---

30 ml (2 tbsp) double cream

---

1. Turn the yogurt into a muslin-lined sieve and place over a bowl. Leave for 24 hours until whey has dripped through to bowl leaving a thickened yogurt.

2. Turn the yogurt into a separate bowl and stir in the cream. Refrigerate until needed.

——— COOK'S TIP ———
If you do not have any muslin, line the sieve with a double thickness of disposable kitchen cloth.

SAVOURY BUTTER

A generous slice of savoury butter can cheer up the cheapest piece of fish and enhance the choicest sole or turbot. What's more it can be made ahead and kept in the freezer as an ever convenient supply. Below is the traditional lemon and parsley recipe plus some less obvious alternatives.

Makes about 100 g (4 oz)

---

100 g (4 oz) butter

---

zest of 1 lemon

---

30 ml (2 level tbsp) chopped parsley

---

salt and freshly ground black pepper

---

1. Place the butter in a bowl and beat well until softened.

2. Beat in the lemon zest, parsley and seasoning.

3. Form the mixture into a sausage shape and roll up in greaseproof or foil. Refrigerate or freeze until required.

4. Serve cut into slices.

——— VARIATION ———
Substitute one of the following for the lemon and parsley:

Citrus: Add the grated zest of 1 orange or lime and 10 ml (2 tsp) of the juice.

Garlic Prawn: Drain 50–70 g (2–3 oz) peeled prawns on kitchen paper. Chop then pound to a smooth paste. Add to the softened butter with 1 crushed garlic clove.

Smoked Salmon: Chop and then pound 50–70 g (2–3 oz) smoked salmon to a smooth paste. Add to the softened butter with 2.5 ml ($\frac{1}{2}$ level tsp) grated lemon zest.

Curried: Add 2.5 ml ($\frac{1}{2}$ level tsp) curry paste and 1.5 ml ($\frac{1}{4}$ level tsp) fresh chopped coriander.

Mustard: Add 10–15 ml (2–3 level tsp) coarse grain mustard.

MAYONNAISE

Although there is an ever broadening array of mayonnaises on display at the supermarket or grocers, homemade is always superior and despite popular belief, easily prepared after one attempt.

This quantity makes plenty and keeps for a week in the refrigerator, even if flavoured with one of the variations below.

Makes about 350 ml (12 fl oz)

2 large egg yolks
15 ml (1 tbsp) white wine vinegar
salt and freshly ground black pepper
300 ml (½ pint) olive oil

1. Place the yolks in a liquidizer or food processor with the vinegar and a little seasoning.

2. Blend until the ingredients are combined. Pour the oil very slowly onto the eggs, blending continuously until thick and pale.

3. Add more seasoning if necessary and store in the refrigerator. (If the mixture should curdle place another egg yolk into the cleaned liquidizer and gradually blend in the curdled mixture.)

VARIATION

To half the quantity of mayonnaise try one of the following variations for accompanying plainer cooked fish, salads and shellfish.

Tartare Sauce: Stir in a small handful of finely chopped parsley, 30 ml (2 level tbsp) finely chopped gherkins and 30 ml (2 level tbsp) chopped capers.

Aioli: Add 2–3 skinned and crushed garlic cloves.

Green Mayonnaise: Pound together 5 ml (1 level tsp) each of watercress, parsley or chervil, tarragon and chives. Blanch 25 g (1 oz) spinach or sorrel leaves in boiling water. Thoroughly drain and finely chop. Beat into the mayonnaise with the pounded mixture.

Pink Mayonnaise: Stir in 30 ml (2 level tbsp) tomato purée and a good pinch of ground paprika.

INDEX

INDEX